Some Unrecognized Factors in MEDICINE

Some Unrecognized Factors in MEDICINE

Edited by
H. TUDOR EDMUNDS
and ASSOCIATES

A QUEST BOOK

Published under a grant from the Kern Foundation

THE THEOSOPHICAL PUBLISHING HOUSE
Wheaton, Ill., U.S.A.
Madras, India / London, England

Originally published by The Theosophical Publishing House, London.

First Quest Edition published by the Theosophical Publishing House, Wheaton, Illinois, a department of The Theosophical Society in America, 1976

Library of Congress Cataloging in Publication Data
Main entry under title:

Some unrecognized factors in medicine.

  (A Quest book)
  Bibliography: p.
  Includes index.
  1. Therapeutic systems. 2. Medicine, Psychosomatic.
3. Medicine, Hindu. I. Edmunds, Henry Tudor. [DNLM:
1. Therapeutic cults. WB960 E24s]
R753.S65   1976   610   75-28092
ISBN 0-8356-0471-3

Printed in the United States of America

TABLE OF CONTENTS

There are two classes of disease—bodily and mental. Each arises from the other. Neither is perceived to exist without the other. Of a truth mental disorders arise from physical ones, and likewise physical disorders arise from mental ones.

Mahabharata: Santi Parva, xvi, 8-9.

PREFACE TO THE SECOND EDITION

This book was compiled from notes made by the Medical Group of the Theosophical Research Centre, London, over a number of years. During its career the group had a shifting membership, but there were four who remained throughout, and who are therefore responsible for the actual text of the first edition, and for the revisions to be found in this, the second edition of the book. Two of the four are medically qualified, one being in general practice, the other a psychotherapist; two are not, but practise as lay psychotherapists, each one having special qualifications for taking part in work of this kind. No names appeared in the first edition, but it has been felt that, as a matter of policy, the names of those principally concerned should be made known. They are Laurence J. Bendit, M.D., D.P.M.; Phoebe D. Bendit; H. Tudor Edmunds, M.B., B.S.; E. Adelaide Gardner, B.A.. M. Beddow Bayly, M.R.C.S., L.R.C.P., wrote the section on bacterial theory. To all other members, both medical and lay, who from time to time participated in the discussions, this group records its thanks.

The text of this edition has been considerably revised. It is only fair to ourselves to say that, had time permitted, we should have preferred to rewrite it altogether: in over ten years one's style, if not one's views, have of necessity changed. But while certain views expressed in 1939 have been modified during the war years, it is satisfactory that most of the basic material presented in the first edition still holds good, so that in the rewriting it would have been more a matter of presenting things differently than of any very fundamental change of attitude. Certain additions have been made: chemotherapy did not exist on any large scale before the war, nor had electrical convulsion therapy and prefontal leucotomy been invented.

7

It is hoped that anything savouring of didacticism has been rigorously excluded from the book. Should this not have been done let it be said that the writers are fully aware of the need for an open and flexible mind, and a tentative approach to any subject such as that here discussed. It should be added also that, though the writers are agreed on fundamentals, not all of them are in sympathy with every view contained in the text. There are many points on which a "minority report" would show a distinctly different attitude from that which has been incorporated. The basic ideas, moreover, are not confined to personal experience. They are also to be found in traditional writings, but it is freely admitted that much has also been included that the writers have found useful in practice, but which on modern scientific standards is as yet quite unproven.

Chapter I

INTRODUCTION

In presenting this book to the public a few words of explanation in regard to its origin and purpose may be helpful. The book is the work of a group of students who met regularly to study the problems of health and disease in the light of certain eastern teachings on these subjects. It was felt that as medical teaching and practice in both East and West were the result of a serious and scientific approach to the problem of health, much might be gained by an attempt to align the older theories of Hindu tradition, in particular, with some of the modern western theories. The group was familiar with and open to both these lines of thought: it was felt that each had valuable material to provide which might possibly be complementary. This was found to be the case.

The actual writing of the book served a twofold purpose. First, in dealing with so vast and intricate a subject it was obviously necessary to follow a definite scheme of study in order to prevent digression and waste of energy. Accordingly, a beginning was made by selecting headings roughly based on those of the ordinary medical curriculum in which anatomy and physiology are the groundwork and diagnosis and treatment constitute the later stages. Further, it was agreed that the writing down of conclusions would help to make them clear and objective and therefore avoid vagueness and lack of logical continuity.

The group was soon involved in a recurrent comparison between the vitalistic and the mechanistic attitudes towards the problems of disease and healing. The second purpose of the book became that of presenting the viewpoint of the writers in such a form as to make clear the

9

contrast between their approach to the subject and the materialistic approach which is still often taught in medical schools. The medical student normally learns much that is purely objective in anatomy, physiology, pathology, chemistry and so on, and is then sent out into practice equipped with this and little else. Before long he finds that he has forgotten three-quarters of what he learned, and either sinks into a routine use of the remaining quarter or else utilizes the space cleared by this removal of unneeded facts into the lumber-room of his mind to begin to learn the practice of his art. It has been said that a good practitioner never again feels as omniscient as on the day when he passes his final examination, since thenceforward he finds himself faced by problem after problem which is not to be solved by book knowledge alone. Thus he is thrown back upon himself, and it is a well-known fact that the best physician or healer is not necessarily the one with the greatest number of degrees and honours, but rather one who is sensitive and intuitive and who makes the closest and most sympathetic contact with his patient's personality.

It is hoped that this book may offer a line of approach more adequate than the two-dimensional one of purely materialistic medical science. It may even help to a deeper understanding of the patient and explain much that is ignored or discounted when man is looked upon as a physical body only.

The group is fully aware that the survey made has been cursory. It was agreed, however, to make a preliminary survey of the whole ground rather than to specialize on some particular disease or treatment. This present work may be regarded as a small-scale map of the general field of eastern occultism in relation to medical practice, based, as it were, upon a first triangulation of the land and nothing more. If the general plan is more or less accurate, however, it will be found that later and more detailed investigations will fit into it.

The writers are also fully conscious of the fact that this

is by no means a scientific work in the ordinary sense in which the West understands that word, for, from the western viewpoint, much in it must be taken as 'not proven'. Nothing, however, that is purely traditional has been stated without labelling it as such, while many of the facts cited have been arrived at through years of observation, from a somewhat different angle than that usually taken, of ordinary clinical cases. If the statements made read strangely to those unfamiliar with this angle of approach we can only say that they are conclusions drawn from experience and are so presented for examination; further proof and corrections will come in due course.

In the meantime it is hoped that this general outline may be found to be at least hypothetically sound by those who are prepared, on occasion, to allow the intellectual desire for objective proof of a statement to be put aside in favour of the testimony of the intuitive sense. The intuition frequently gives one a peculiar perception about a situation which may or may not, at the moment, be supported by material evidence. Yet, if the concept is truly sensed by the intuitive faculty, scientific demonstration will be achieved at a later period.

It is by no means unscientific to accept certain concepts as working hypotheses. We ask the reader to take this attitude in regard to the findings derived from extra-sensory perception, and unsupported by other means, on which some of the contents of this book are based. Extra-sensory perception is now being established 'to a high degree of (mathematical) probability', notably since the experiments made in France and America, which have followed those recorded by Rhine.[1] It is nowadays quite in order in scientific circles, when writing a paper on some psycho-physical subject, to begin with the assumption that the existence of 'the psi function' in telepathy, clairvoyance, etc., is already proved. Thus, for our part, we do not propose to explain or elaborate this aspect of our research work or experience. Those who are unfamiliar with the use of psychic faculty in diagnosis and in other matters of health are asked to investigate the possibility and uses of extra-sensory perception as an independent study, or to accept it for the moment as an hypothesis.

In regard to the terminology used, although for many points an accepted vocabulary already exists, for certain other aspects of this research we have been obliged to find new names. Every growing science develops a new set of terms as its concepts become more explicit: the vitalistic approach to health is no exception. Where ordinary English or accepted technical expressions convey the meaning satisfactorily these have been used, but in some cases no current western terminology adequately fits the facts. In such cases, if an eastern or theosophical word already conveys an explicit concept, such as that covered by the term 'prāna', we have adopted it.

The chief divergence between the view here presented and that of ordinary science is that, in the light of the findings of science itself, a purely mechanistic idea of man seems to the writers to be no longer tenable. On the other hand there is much in modern science, psychology and psychic research to support the view they advance.[2] For example, psychic research has demonstrated that thought and feeling can go on apart from the body. This is true not only in trance phenomena, where the subject is apparently able to be active at a great distance from where his body lies, but probably also in purely psychic conditions when the physical body is dead and destroyed.

Again, man does not depend altogether on his five senses to obtain knowledge and impressions. Introspective experiments in psychological laboratories have opened up new fields of investigation on these lines.[3] There are also a number of instances on record which strongly suggest that something active and conscious and able to remember has passed out of a dead body and been reborn into another body as a baby.[4] This would mean that reincarnation is possible, although no proof as yet exists of the widely held belief that it is a general law. If it is true, an individual human being is not his body only, but must be thought of as active and conscious in non-physical spheres.

Moreover, psychology has found itself confronted by the wealth of phenomena connected with religious and spiritual experience, and by the remarkable significance that these have, both for the individual and for the race. It is no longer content to label these as 'hysteria'—a useful word with which to dismiss what one does not understand—nor is it content to disregard as merely superstitious, religious and legendary traditions and the folk-lore of the ancient and the primitive. It has, indeed, become quite orthodox in certain scientific and psychological circles to speak of the soul and to use the term 'spiritual'.

But while scientists are becoming more aware of these matters, they have not yet progressed beyond the study of psychic phenomena in terms of function. There is so far no indication of the exact sphere in which the phenomena take place. To many, the mind and the psychic functions exist only as abstractions with no real or objective existence in the space-time continuum. It is here that the theosophical scheme, drawn from many ancient sources, supplies a convenient theory or hypothesis concerning the material though subtle mechanisms by which a man feels, thinks, receives inspirational ideas, and wills.

Although this theory describes a mechanism, it starts from the opposite basis to that of mechanistic materialism, being essentially vitalistic. A comparison between this view and that of the modern orthodox scientist in regard to man may be summed up by saying that modern science still looks upon man as being a body with, perhaps, a soul or spirit tacked on to it somewhere, while the student of the ancient sciences holds that man is a spirit which, for its own purposes and from time to time, attaches a body or bodies to itself and uses these as instruments whereby to receive stimuli and to act in the material world. According to the ancient tradition, also, everything except the eternal spirit of man is considered to have some degree of objective extension in space-time. The soul, or mind, is thus an object in space—a view not proved, but nevertheless in no way inconsistent with any positive findings in modern psychology.

It is the clear-cut acceptance of the objectivity of these bodies and of the superphysical worlds in which they function that constitutes the most marked divergence between the eastern approach to psychology and medicine and that of the West.

We do not, however, propose in this transaction to go into the arguments for or against the objectivity of what is often regarded as purely subjective experience. We frankly use an objective terminology because the phenomena with which we are dealing are best defined in these terms. If such terms, again, are accepted by the reader merely as best expressing the hypotheses under consideration, there need be no misunderstanding.

We shall speak of the *physical body*, that part of man, known to us all, which consists of solid, liquid and gaseous matter, and in the study of which we include the physical organs and their functions.

The phrase, the *vital body*,[5] will be used as an omnibus term to cover those phenomena of a vital nature which have to do with radiation resulting from chemical changes in cells; with the vital discharges known as nervous impulses;[6] with all that is conveyed to westerners by such words as vitality, animal magnetism, or vital energy, and to eastern students by the term 'personal prāna'. Of this vital body we shall have much to say for it holds the key to many problems which are under investigation to-day. The work that is being done upon the positive and negative electrons within the body, changes in bodily potential, and the electrical capacity of the body, all falls within the field covered by this term. The function and description of this subtle and vital aspect of the human mechanism will be dealt with later. Its chief activities are two: (1) to act as a subtle matrix for all physiological changes, as the organizer wherein the pattern of the new structure lies, as a vital centre whence directive energies are variously distributed through the more mechanical chemical components of blood, organs and tissues; and (2) to act as a bridge mechanism linking the non-physical aspects of man with the actual physical structure. A 'live' body possesses such a bridge mechanism and vital matrix. In a dead body the bridge has been broken. When there is no longer the unifying influence of the thinker, i.e. the spiritual self behind the act of thought, holding the constituent parts in some sort of co-operative relationship, these fall apart into inco-ordination and disintegration ensues.

The Psychic Body

The *emotional nature*, frequently called the astral body in modern occult literature, has little structural form of its own, although its register of wave-lengths is said to be clearly defined and to lie between those of the finest physical material and the densest mental matter. The active energy of this level playing through the vital body from the physical sensorium, is experienced as sensation. It likewise constantly plays through personal mental images, and is then experienced as feeling, emotion and passion.

The *mental body*, by contrast, is a clear-cut, structured organism, within which all personal thought-processes take place. Hence it is far more readily analyzed and comprehended than the fluidic ebb and flow of the emotional nature.

In ordinary people the two levels of experience—emotional and intellectual—are so interlocked that they constitute a single functional unit, although certain well established practices of self-analysis and self-discipline enable their distinctive pattern-formations to be studied. The mental and the emotional natures may well be compared to electricity and magnetism which differ in quality and behave differently, though they are always found in association.

Careful investigation will show that many phenomena of automatic behaviour, hypnosis, suggestion and so on, as well as those of a purely psychic character, are capable of strictly scientific interpretation if the substantial nature of the subtler bodies, and of the wave-lengths of thought and feeling of which they are composed and to which they respond, is allowed as an hypothesis.

The bodies mentioned above—physical, vital, mental-emotional—constitute the mask or personality, with a central separative sense of egoism as the chief integrative factor. Behind this mask of the personal factors of ordinary human consciousness lie other and yet subtler principles.[7] For the latter we shall reserve the word *Self*, with a capital 'S'. This is the spiritual man, the permanent centre of experience for each individual human being.[8]

In ordinary life, the Self is usually very little known or noted by the waking consciousness of the physical brain, but its emergence at times into waking life can be startling, and its significance to the psychologist, to the student of comparative religion, of scientific introspection and of yoga, is becoming more and more clearly recognized. The value of this concept in dealing with subtler cases of chronic disease and of psychological disorder will be dealt with in the course of the book.

The writers also accept, in general, the monistic concept that all phenomena of manifestation arise from one central life-principle, whether it be called solar energy, cosmic force or Divine Life. Hence each individual, as an aspect or out-thrust of that life, is at some level of his being indissolubly linked to every other, and in his individualized consciousness is evolving, developing, through many repetitions and varieties of experience, towards an ultimate knowledge of the fact that his life is integrally one with that of his fellows. In modern parlance, each human unit is ever moving towards a larger realization of ultimate reality and of the relation of the phenomena of personal, limited experience to the noumenon, the whole, the meaning within the appearance.[9]

The bearing of all this upon problems of health and disease will appear more clearly as the study proceeds.

It is from such a general standpoint that the chapters which follow have been written. In times past, treatment by nostrums and witchcraft came to be superseded by that based upon observed facts and scientific accuracy. To-day it is becoming evident that the tide of thought which, in regard to medical as well as other science, had ebbed into a limited materialism, is now flowing back over the old ground, bringing with it a rational and scientific interpretation of much that has hitherto been regarded as purely superstitious. This group is by no means alone in pushing investigation into the realm of the psyche and of the subjective in a search for the cause of disease conditions in the physical body. Within the rising tide of a socialized and spiritualized scientific outlook, and with the help of a new interpretation, the subjective experience of man as we are now describing it can and should become a field for the strictest scientific investigation. For this highly specialized research new methods of approach are required and will have to be evolved: introspection, such as Aveling and others have used; the intuitive faculty; and other extra-sensory methods of investigation which are still rare as trained capacities. The group has been fortunate in being able, for the purpose of this study, to make use of workers who possess the rare gift of trained psychic capacity, and clairvoyance in particular has been used when available as a useful cross-check upon introspective investigation, side by side with the more usual and external methods of observation and research. If the inclusion of such observers is startling to some readers, we merely ask them to consider the results upon their merits, as hypotheses to be tested further.

In conclusion, we repeat that what follows is put forward tentatively and will doubtless be subject, as time goes on, to continued reconsideration.

No. Page

1   11   J. B. Rhine: *New Frontiers of the Mind*. Faber & Faber.
           J. B. Rhine: *Extra-Sensory Perception*. Faber & Faber.
           J. B. Rhine: *The Reach of the Mind*. Faber & Faber.
           Charles Richet: Review of above, *British Medical Journal*,
               October 1935.
           Alexis Carrel: *Man, the Unknown*, pp. 124, 126. Hamish
               Hamilton.
           See also recurrent references to recent experiment in peri-
               odicals such as those of the Society for Psychical Research,
               the *Journal of Parapsychology* and other scientific bodies.
           Earlier literature on this subject:
           von Schrenck-Notzing: *Phenomena of Materialisation*. Kegan
               Paul & Trench.
           Gustave Geley: *From the Unconscious to the Conscious*. Collins.
           Eugene Ostey: *Supernormal Faculties in Man*. Methuen.

2   12   Gerald Heard: *The Third Morality*, Chapters II, IV, V, VI.
               Castle.
           Francis Aveling: *Psychology: The Changing Outlook*. Watts.

3   12   *Journal of Parapsychology*, Vol. I, No. 1. March 1937,
               pp. 1-9. Duke University Press, Durham, U.S.A.

4   13   Ralph Shirley: *The Problem of Rebirth*. Rider.

5   14   This term is used in place of the classical one, *etheric body*.
               Not only does it adequately describe what it means where
               man's constitution is concerned, but it is more in tune with
               scientific thought which has dethroned the old concept of
               the ether of space in favour of more modern hypotheses.

6   14   George Crile: *The Phenomena of Life*. Heinemann.
           A. V. Hill: 'The Physical Nature of the Nerve Impulse',
               Nature, Vol. CXXXI, Jan.-Feb. 1933. Presidential
               address.

7   16   Geraldine Coster: *Yoga and Western Psychology*, Chapters
               VI and XV. Oxford University Press.

8   16   Francis Aveling: *Outline of Modern Knowledge*, pp. 342, 343.
               Victor Gollancz.

9   17   Aldous Huxley: *Ends and Means*, pp. 253-6. Chatto & Windus.

Chapter II

THE RELATION BETWEEN PHYSICIAN AND
PATIENT

IN the opening session of our group discussions, considerable time was spent in attempting to discern and to define the relationship between doctor and patient that is most conductive to the patient's permanent recovery from illness; that is, the relationship that helps to produce real healing.

It was agreed that the modern specialist has great advantages over earlier practitioners in having readily available the vast amount of detailed information supplied by modern methods of clinical investigation. This gives him very direct knowledge of the conditions under which the bodily organism of his patient is functioning. On the other hand, the old-fashioned 'family doctor' possessed equally important advantages that modern highly specialized consultants too often lack. The general practitioner of the old school was usually on personal terms with his patients and combined the work of confessor, family adviser and medical specialist. He had a view of his patient as a whole—psyche, physical body and environment—and so could frame an accurate picture of the subtle pressures that were inducing diseased conditions in the physical organism.[1]

The modern highly-trained consultant may have only one brief interview with the patient, and has to form his estimate of the case largely from a chart prepared by others, which presents in extremely significant detail the picture of the patient's metabolic and chemical pattern. It is true that he views the patient with a fresh mind, while the family doctor may have 'gone stale' on it, but while this gives him a better opportunity than the local practitioner is likely to have of seeing the patient in correct perspective, such a specialist often fails to obtain a complete picture of the patient by altogether omitting the psychological and spiritual factors. Such conditions as calcium deficiency can occur for many reasons, as will be shown later, and the administration of calcium in assimilable form is difficult. It is doubtful if an aberrant thyroid is ever satisfactorily dealt with by massive doses of thyroid extract; and while certain putrefactive flora in the intestines may be damped down by the administration of kaolin or sulphonamides, they frequently recur when the dose is stopped, showing that the basic cause of their development has not been touched.

At the present time the growth of interest in certain psychological factors, as tending to create a predisposition to disease, shows the trend of modern medicine to be turning away from the purely chemical and mechanical view of metabolic problems.[2] Constitutional or individual medicine is coming more and more into favour, and there is a growing recognition that the clinical picture of the individual, his personal metabolic pattern, including endocrine activities, assimilation, excretion and the rest, is incomplete unless there is added an appreciation of the psychological type, and of those psychological conditions which, at the very least, may be said always to accompany the physiological pattern.

Yet if the psyche is to re-enter the picture, there needs to be a return, whenever possible, to the old family doctor relationship between patient and physician. The typical family doctor was often, as we have said, confessor as well as physician, with special opportunities for noticing significant details, personal and environmental, affecting his patient's health. And he frequently possessed a happy midway attitude between that of the priest and that of the doctor alone.

The approach of the priest to a visitor coming for advice is to view him as a soul with an illusory body attached, whereas the average doctor tends to view his patient as a body with an hypothetical set of psychological mechanisms. The view of the classical priest-physician, and one which has been found to be most successful in the clinical practice of members of this group, is that in which the patient is recognized primarily as a unique spiritual entity. This entity is seen as deeply involved in his psychological and physical mechanisms, with body and mind functioning closely together, almost as a single organism. The disturbance of the body is only a part of the problem presented, and to deal with the situation successfully, so that real health can result, the doctor should try to see the patient as a whole.

We do not wish to pause here and argue the question of the recognition of the spiritual factor. It may be considered purely as an hypothesis by those who are unfamiliar with or unsympathetic to this approach. But there are many who know that there is a mysterious and imponderable force which may save a case, and the absence of which may easily lose it. Many names are given to this factor—stamina, the will to live, nervous vitality—but whatever it is, it enables the patient to co-operate with the efforts of the physician and nurses, or of the psychologist, and so assists the body to pull through.

The problem of the doctor who desires a relatively permanent cure for his patient is closely involved with the problem of vitality and stamina, and to deal with this adequately he must obtain a full picture of the patient in three aspects. The physiological data, the biochemical analyses and other specialized forms of laboratory diagnosis are of very great assistance and significance in building up this picture. The physiological chart is one factor—a factor of paramount importance—because it is the physical body that the physician is expected to heal. The other two factors are the psyche, with its problems, and the individual as a spiritual entity with a certain destiny and purpose of his own.

With this third factor the physician in ordinary

practice may have little to do, but every doctor knows the case in which it may suddenly leap to the front and become of the greatest significance. That such cases are still frequently treated with ignorant or shallow indifference to the deeper issues involved is perhaps one reason for the increase of chronic nervous disease and even of insanity.

The mind-body mechanism works as a whole, and illness is a patent indication of maladjustment not only in the physical body but throughout the whole nature. While most orthodox practitioners tend to regard disease as a foreign entity to be removed by medical skill, we would regard disease primarily as the direct result of mistakes made by the patient himself, and only to be *finally* eradicated by a readjustment on his part in reference to his personal life and environment.

The body may be healthy in itself when the physiological mechanism is working harmoniously, but to be permanently in good health a person must have made an harmonious adjustment to his environment *at all levels*, and one that is suitable to his stage of evolutionary development. Otherwise the seeds of disorder are present and may at any moment become active in terms of bodily disease. Naturally at periods of transition and rapid psychological change physical disorder occurs very easily, but far less easily if the child or adult is happy in his growth-process.

The means of interaction between psyche and body will be more fully dealt with in later chapters. Here we are considering the attitude of the doctor to his patient. The orthodox doctor, if asked, will say that he regards the symptoms presented in a given case as a problem to be solved by the use of his own knowledge and intelligence, a sort of crossword puzzle to be elucidated by his own brain mechanism. The approach we are aiming at attempts to induce the patient consciously to uncover in himself the deeper cause of his own trouble, with the doctor's help. This may be termed assisting the patient to discover the relation of his real Self to his symptoms. It is necessary, however, to realize that there will always be a portion of the patient's nature, conscious or unconscious, that does not wish to find this out, because for this bit of himself, the illness has some use. There will always be many patients who, despite protests to the contrary, do not really want to get well.

For all usual cases, except in those trivial or specific difficulties for which there is an immediate solution, the doctor's chief concern in the early interview should be to secure the co-operation of the patient both in arriving at an understanding of the causes of ill-health and in following the course of treatment indicated.

To gain this co-operation it is obviously essential to build an open and friendly relationship which functions as a bridge between the doctor and the patient. This has to be an individual matter, and the approach will naturally have to be different in every case. Sometimes the question-and-answer method, inevitable in most early interviews, forms an excellent basis for such bridge-building. The very thoroughness of the questions as to what the patient eats and how he sleeps can breed confidence if they are rightly put, but at other times this may be better avoided in favour of a purely friendly first contact, in which the patient is made to feel that he is considered primarily as a human being and not as a case or a specimen under a microscope.

An underrated factor in securing co-operation is that of being willing, at least to some extent, to explain to the patient the nature of the medicine advised and the purpose of the treatment. Some doctors believe in absolute silence on these matters, in a sort of doctrine of infallibility, and give the prescription or bottle with a dictum 'This will do you good' or 'This is what you need' —both admirable psychological suggestions. But while this technique may work effectively with a physician who has established a reputation for success, or who possesses a potent personality, or with certain suggestible patients, many are sceptical in such matters and want to understand what is wrong with themselves and how it is being treated. For all such persons frankness is invaluable, whenever possible, as it is also in other cases, because of its effect on the doctor-patient relationship.

The actual knowledge of bodily conditions, family history, psychological tendencies, etc., to be gained in the course of early interviews with a patient are tabulated and discussed in the chapter on diagnosis. Here we are concerned with the physician himself and with the mode of his approach.

Whereas the physiological problems presented in clinical work always demand the keenest intellectual analysis, there are certain subtle factors in a difficult case that only make themselves known to what we must call, for lack of a more definite term, the intuitive mind. In our scheme of approach and treatment we are definitely concerned with linking the inner and somewhat obscure factors in disease with a rational and scientific treatment of the physical body. For such work an active and reliable intuition is a great asset. This is usually referred to in medical circles as clinical sense.

The intuition is now recognized in psychology as a normal function of the mind, irrational in so far as it sees around corners and through obstacles, and therefore sometimes cuts across a logical and reasoned argument, based on insufficient data.

It arrives at a true judgment by direct interior contact with concealed factors.[3] It is possible to develop the intuitive approach by cultivating open and quiet habits of mind, which are congenial to the working of the intuitive faculty.

Another quality that is necessary for success in such intimate work is that of goodwill to all patients alike. Make-believe, or just a good bedside manner, will not establish the relationship desired nor permit the intuition to function reliably. The unconscious, if not the conscious mind of the patient is always affected and reacts to insincerity, however well disguised. Even if outwardly the patient seems gratified by it, something in him is left unsatisfied. Naturally, every practitioner has good and bad days, of fatigue and strain, of ease and delight in the work, but a certain equilibrium in outlook can and should be cultivated if the inner side of healing and medical work is to be wisely handled.

This is a counsel of perfection, and the good physician who is conscious of a present limitation does not hesitate nor feel it derogatory to his self-respect to refer certain patients to other physicians when he feels he is temperamentally incapable of dealing with them.

The sound physician is naturally more interested in health than in disease. It is also obvious that he needs to have experienced health and some measure of psychological balance in his own personality if he is to assist his patient to achieve these conditions in himself. It is by no means a bar to good work for the physician to have bodily or emotional or mental problems to deal with in himself, provided he is aware of them and is prepared to deal with them constructively. It does not matter if he is continually defeated by the conditions of his life in his attempt to achieve freedom from worry, overwork or pressing responsibility. What is necessary is that he should have arrived, or be intent upon arriving, within himself, at a solution of his problem, not expecting an external deity or the forces of nature to alter those circumstances for his convenience.

This acceptance of life as a problem to be solved by himself is essential. All resources at hand may be used and others sought as need arises, but nevertheless he should expect, by a process of continued growth and self-change, to be able to arrive at some sort of working adjustment between his personality and the problems presented by his own environment. The physician can *convey* his own attitude to life to his patients provided he is simple and sincere, but he cannot hope to impose it on them by intellectual argument or homily unsupported by evidence of a deep application of these arguments to his own way of living.

To sum up this chapter briefly, the approach to the patient which conduces to real healing is one in which the physician, while using the best knowledge and technique that modern medical science can offer or that he can command, co-ordinates this with a picture of the patient as a whole, spirit, mind and body, and envisages the patient's problem in the light of all three of these factors. To achieve this the intuitive faculty may have to be cultivated. In the process of cultivating this, and of using the technique suggested, the doctor will meet and must deal with his own problems.

If the patient is to be healed rather than patched up, the doctor has to develop in himself a certain integration which will give him a healing quality. The physician who desires to be a true healer, to assist his patient to harmonize the mind as well as the body, should be willing to train his own mind to this end. It is obvious that in the course of such a training of himself he will learn much that is of the utmost value in the understanding of his patients.

NOTES AND REFERENCES FOR CHAPTER II

No.	Page	
1	20	A. Campbell Stark: *An Index to General Practice;* section under 'Introduction'. Baillière, Tindall & Cox.
2	21	E. M. Westburgh: *Introduction to Clinical Psychology.* P. Blakiston & Co. Inc. Philadelphia, 1937.
3	25	C. G. Jung: *Psychological Types.* Kegan Paul.

Chapter III

THE PATIENT

THE PHYSICAL, VITAL AND SUBTLER BODIES

GENERAL REMARKS. Under the above heading we shall attempt to give a picture of the patient in his threefold nature, as indicated in the introductory chapter. Traditional eastern teachings contain interesting material describing the unseen bodies, or structures, used by human consciousness, and their relation to the physical body. We have been able to verify at least some of these, both by inference from treatments given which followed the eastern line of approach and by direct observation on the part of one or more persons who possess and have been trained to use extra-sensory perception.

Although for the sake of clarity it is necessary to divide the material into sections dealing with the different levels of psychological and physiological function, it needs to be remembered always that each individual acts as a body-mind unit, with the consciousness of the inner Self playing through all the psychological levels of mental, emotional and sensory response, and acting as the unifying principle. It is true that intense physical sensation, overwhelming emotion or concentrated thought can bring a momentary experience of unification which is extremely satisfying, but that which experiences, remembers, and persists from day to day as a thread runs through a string of beads, we term the Self. When it is withdrawn, as in death, or partially cut off, as in insanity, the bodies through which the Self normally manifests either disintegrate or fall into confusion of behaviour.[1]

THE PHYSICAL BODY. Very little space need be given to discussion of western views concerning the dense physical body, its organs and functions. Any student not already familiar with orthodox literature on this subject is referred to standard textbooks on physiology, anatomy and bio-chemistry, of which there are many.

Eastern literature dealing with physiological structure and function is scanty, and is written from so radically different a view-point that comparisons are difficult to make. Such writings as are available seem for the most part to be compilations of oral teachings given to students of yoga, or to physicians whose attitude to the problems of medicine was not only vitalistic but often magical and religious. In such literature, the influence of mind upon body is assumed, as is also a vast range of correspondences with astronomical data—such as phases of the moon and the relation of medicines to suitable times of the year—while some information is given concerning the basic temperaments and their tendencies to certain diseases. There is an almost untouched field of research open here, though the available material is limited.[2] Useful work is beginning to be done in India by medical men, some of whom, having been trained in Europe, have found on their return to India that certain of the indigenous forms of medical treatment were better suited to their Indian patients than purely western methods.[3]

It is possible that in time the eastern and western systems may come to be considered as complementary. Western students, viewing the body as a machine, have accumulated an immense mass of information concerning physiological detail, with minute, accurate examination of physical cell structure, the chemistry of metabolic processes, etc. Until very recently, however, they had almost ignored the problem of vitality and the influence of psychological factors upon it.

Eastern traditional literature has very little exact information that tallies with the results of western research, but it contains nothing that contradicts it. It concerns itself almost wholly with the question of vitality, and deals in considerable detail with various vital activities affecting bodily processes, which are all clearly described and differentiated.

There are enumerations and descriptions of a group of organs termed the *nadis*, which control vital functions. This term has been thought by some to be another name for the physical nerves, viewed from a vital and functional angle, but these nadis certainly do not exactly correspond to the nerves of the physical body as investigated by western physiologists.

If, then, the word *nadi* does at all refer to the various nervous systems in the dense physical frame, it will refer to them chiefly as carriers of the subtle vital energy known as *prāna*. This term—*prāna*—will recur constantly, so we must attempt to define it, although the concept is foreign to western views and hence difficult to convey.

Solar energy is recognized by Hindu medical students as the source of all forms of energy within our solar system. Some western students now claim to have observed that, in sunlight, a subtle change occurs in certain otherwise unattached particles in the air which binds them together into a group carrying a charge of a special vital or growth-stimulating force. This group has been termed the *vitality globule*, and is said to be formed only in sunlight. Our observers have also seen it present in large quantities when ultra-violet light was used. The term *free prāna* is used to describe the supply of these vitally-charged groups which exist in the air.

Prāna, in general, means breath or life, and there is a wide range of usage for the word in eastern physiology, in yoga, and in the general theories of occultism. For our purpose we shall confine our use of it to its meaning as biological, or vital, energy, one manifestation of which is the free prāna described above. In behaviour this vital energy is closely allied to electricity, with which it has many characteristics in common, such as positive and negative reactions, but it is different in quality, having an affinity with protoplasm, with a life-enhancing action. To-day, the distinction between electric and biochemical activity is beginning to be recognized, and the existence of the eastern hypothesis of a biochemical energy with its own qualities and laws of behaviour may interest students specializing in these subjects.

In the human body prāna is further specialized by each individual, for it is drawn in as one breathes, through special prānic centres and distributed over the body with incredible rapidity. It thus becomes personal vital energy, or personal vitality.

Modern occult students describe prāna as running along the myelin sheaths of the nerves and not through the nerve fibres themselves. (The latter are said to transmit a type of energy not yet clearly differentiated or understood in the West.) In the eastern view this prāna is the essential vital factor necessary for cell life, and the physical body is built up as an expression of its activity. It uses the nervous system as its line of communication throughout the body, in the same way that the arteries and veins are used as the chief means for the circulation of the blood; and just as the blood plasma itself seeps out as lymph into every cell of the body, so also this vital energy, prāna, is by no means confined to the nervous system, but is present in every cell and molecule of living forms.[4]

The importance of the condition of the nervous system in determining healthy or diseased conditions is daily receiving more consideration in the West, as the work of McDonagh, Crile and others testifies.[5] It would seem that this fact has long ago been recognized in the Hindu school of medicine.

Prāna also has a special connection with the endocrine glands, as we shall suggest in more detail later. Its flow is automatically responsive to the psychological state of the individual, so that the study of prāna and its behaviour as a bridging influence linking the psyche to the body may in future give the key to certain mysteries of endocrinology.

The nerves, then, are of the greatest importance in occult physiology, because they act as carriers of prāna, the essence of physical vitality. Through the response of prāna to the subjective life of the individual the sympathetic, the para-sympathetic and the cortical levels of the cerebro-spinal systems are each linked to special psychological aspects of animal and human consciousness. The sympathetic nervous system reacts directly, as is now well known, to emotion; the cerebro-spinal at its highest levels, i.e. above the optic thalamus, reacts to conscious thought through the cerebral cortex, and to many unconscious states probably through the basal ganglia and notably through the hypothalamus. The para-sympathetic nervous system is just now coming into its own in the West as a field of study. The eastern teaching relates it in its functional activity to the selective, balancing, and creative capacities of the psyche. The most significant nerve in the body, from this view-point, is the vagus, called the 'Vina of Shiva' in eastern literature.[6] The inhibiting and balancing functions of the vagal system in relation to the sympathetic and cerebro-spinal systems are now known to western physiologists, as well as something of its relation to endocrine activity. Jacobson's work with deliberately induced relaxation,[7] indicates that the function of this nerve, has not been exaggerated. It is only recently, however, that we in the West have had sufficiently detailed knowledge of its relation and of the relation of the para-sympathetic system as a whole to metabolism to be able to compare our physiological, empirical findings with the equally detailed but different information given in the eastern literature.

Once more the comparison is made difficult by the fact that the East approaches the problem of metabolism almost entirely from the vital, and not from the mechanical or chemical, view-point; but here the study of endocrinology helps us, and it is by emphasizing the balancing activities of the sympathetic and para-sympathetic nervous systems that the nearest approach can be made.[8] Though using entirely different terminologies, both eastern and western physiologists agree that a healthily working body is one in which the metabolic process is functioning in such a way that incoming and outgoing energies are balanced and the nervous energies are unobstructed psychically or physically, so that they can maintain an equilibrium. A clear, scientifically accurate picture of the physiological factors which contribute to metabolic balance or unbalance is one of the best foundations for a study of the methods of approach and treatment that we shall be considering in the later chapters.

THE HUMAN VITAL BODY. In the previous section we have spoken of the absorption of free prāna, or vital energy, by living organisms. This is drawn in by a mechanism which will be described later; it thence travels over the sheaths of the nerves with great rapidity, and is thrown off from all extremities, all orifices, and the pores of the skin. In a healthy body the prānic flow from the body constitutes a fine spray or haze all round it, extending some inches from every surface. There is also a form of static vitality closely associated with the structure of each cell and organ. The interplay of the quick-moving prāna, drawn in from the air, with the static prāna anchored in the cells, constitutes the organism known as the vital body.[9] From one angle, the vital body can be considered as a 'system' of the physical organism, in that it is intimately concerned with the circulation of a particular form of physiological energy—the prāna or vitality. Just as the nervous or vascular systems are present in every part of the body and, if isolated, would give a perfect reproduction of the shape of the body, so if the vital field could be separated from the dense tissues, it too would exactly correspond to the physical form, at any rate as far as its denser layers are concerned.

But this is only half the picture. The vital body is also the bridge over which consciousness travels from the psychic and spiritual individual, through the nervous system to all parts of the dense body in which he lives in the physical world. The vital body thus has a special dual function which makes it different from the mechanical physiological systems which are parts of the dense physical body. The vital field is not such a part but, on the contrary, it is in the nature of a matrix or parent of the physiological organism, which is formed and contained within it.

That which follows is not merely a traditional description, for many of the statements made are based upon fairly recent experiment and observation, both by clairvoyant and clairsentient workers. No authority is claimed for it except the weight of experience upon which it is based.

STRUCTURE AND FUNCTION. Just as each physical body differs from every other, so do vital bodies differ: general principles of structure and function can be given, but they are invariably modified in individual cases. The vital body is a purely physical organism, the particles which form it having a special vital quality. They are subtler than the gaseous in structure, and in their denser manifestations are just visible to ordinary sight under special conditions.[10] The currents of energy which constitute the subtler parts of this 'body' respond to thought, feeling and will with extra-ordinary rapidity, and expand and contract with deep breathing, relaxation and changes of mood. Hence the vital energies are in constant motion and even untrained clairvoyants will often observe clouds of boiling greyish-blue mist shifting over the surface of the dense physical body. Moreover without actually seeing the subtle material it is possible with sensitive fingers to study its quality and variations in tone. 'Etheric touch' as it is called, is natural to some and can be and has been developed by many students to some degree of accuracy. Blind people are particularly sensitive in this way.

The dual function of the vital body is reflected in its structure.

THE DOUBLE. Everything in nature has a subtle physical (etheric) counterpart, inorganic as well as organic struc-

tures being surrounded by this subtle sheath. The difference between the functions of this *double* in organic and
inorganic structures is not yet understood, but as we shall
here be dealing with the human double only this point
does not arise. In the human body every cell, every tissue
and bony structure has its own counterpart of etheric
material anchored to the elements that compose the
structure. The counterpart remains relatively fixed or
stable, acting as the matrix, the organiser or the pattern for
the vital activities inside the cell, organ or tissue with
which it is associated. All vital activities in the interior of
a structure occur, and all vital changes take place, within
this double; it remains identified with its own section of
the body and varies in density according to the density
of the structure within and around which it functions—
bone, ligament, muscle, etc.

Each type of tissue in the body has a different and
characteristic vital counterpart. There is a vital counterpart associated with the blood stream, in which the
minute particles of food and organic matter are represented by shining globules of a subtle nature, evidently
the double of these particles. The blood, although fluid,
is physiologically considered as a tissue, and the vital
counterpart of the blood is also fluid in its quality. But it
is not an energy current quite like those described in the
next section. The latter flow through dense tissue, just as
electricity flows along or through metal, whereas the vital
counterpart of the blood belongs to the blood itself and
flows with it wherever it goes. On the other hand, a
liquid metal like mercury has its own etheric double, or
counterpart, quite apart from any electric current which
may, or may not, flow along the stream of mercury. In
the same way, the subtler etheric currents may, or may
not, flow along the blood as a conductor, quite apart
from the dense vital or etheric counterpart of the actual
physical blood tissue.

The bony structure is also surrounded and interpene-
trated by a close and intricate mesh of etheric material,

finer and more rigid than that of certain other parts of
the body, but with every ridge of bone as well as the soft
vessels and cells of the marrow exactly reproduced.

Each organ as a whole also has its double, made up of
the vital counterparts of the particular structure, and the
whole human form has its exact vital counterpart extending about one quarter to one half an inch outside the
physical skin. The outer edge of the double may be
termed its skin. This can be seen fairly easily by people
with ordinary sight who will take the necessary trouble
to learn the knack of using the eyes for the purpose:
though near-sighted people usually have more difficulty
than those who are far-sighted.[11] It has the appearance
of a rapidly moving greyish band flowing over the surface
of the physical skin.

THE SUBTLER PRĀNAS. From the etheric skin a series of
emanations are given off, the exact nature of which is not
understood. This is the health aura which Dr. Kilner and
others have described and which many clairvoyants see;
it is only just beyond the range of ordinary long-sighted
vision. It is made up of very rapidly-moving subtle physical material, and an illusion of stability arises from the
speed of movement within the structures. The type of
illusion is familiar, since any fountain or jet of water
appears to have a definite outline, in spite of the intense
activity of the particles forming its shape.

The degree of activity of these subtle radiations depends
somewhat upon the cell structure of the body and of the
double, but even more upon the mind and emotion of the
individual, his psyche, and the way in which his psychological nature affects his breathing: for the flow of these
subtler prānas is directly affected by the breath, and almost
as directly influenced by psychological states. Here we
shall merely describe the appearance of an ordinary
health aura, using this term to describe the subtler
emanations which extend beyond the more static double.

At the edge of the skin of the double—which, as has
been said, is about a quarter to half an inch away from the

physical body—subtle radiations which look like shimmering air above a hot stove can be seen. These are probably actual discharges from or intakes into the various systems of the body. Roughly speaking, the first radiations seen outside the double are pinkish in tone and extend several inches away from the body; they fade out into a mauve area that interpenetrates the pink. Beyond this and yet also interpenetrating the whole vital structure are opalescent emanations and a vast network of fine moonlight-coloured hair-like tubes appearing to originate from the spinal cord and to be associated with the white stream of energy that rises from the base of the spine in the human being and is connected with the spiritual life and the will of man. The physical phenomenon most nearly suggesting the appearance of the vital body and its radiations is probably the aurora borealis in which subtle waves of movement occur, almost colourless, and yet suffused with ethereal and infinitely delicate tones of rose or mauvy light.

There is a great deal of work to be done in studying these vital structure currents and radiations. In health the radiations stand out at right angles to the surface of the body, throwing out surplus or used vitality from the double, while in disease and fatigue they droop and become tangled. Tangled spots due to local disorder can hold back the circulation of prāna, or vitality, and congestion of vitality then takes place locally. When fatigue is general or a condition of fever exists congestion occurs throughout the body, together with disorganization of prāna, including the emanations.

Pain apparently occurs at the point where tangled streams of vital energy have formed an effective block to vital circulation, the strain of the dammed-up energy behind the block bringing about in the dense physical body a certain nervous pressure which causes pain. Moving pains, and spontaneous but transitory itches and skin tension, buzzing in the ear, and sometimes lights before the eyes, which so puzzle the physician, are generally due to shifts in vital pressure, not usually to any actual disease of physical tissues, though they always indicate disturbance either of mind or body.

The skin or edge of the double has an intricate structure. Traditionally it is said to be seven-fold. It is the containing barrier or guardian wall of the double and exists in a state of high tension. There is a well-recognized interchange of material between the physical body and its environment through the physical skin: a similar interchange takes place between the vital body and its vital environment; this occurs far more readily than in the case of the dense body, because of the plastic nature of vital matter. In health these incoming and outgoing forces are held in a state of balance and lead to the healthy metabolism of the body. Injury such as a burn or cut, undue dirt and other incidents, may make a rift in the etheric skin, and psychological attitudes often result in etheric leakage, the patient vaguely 'losing vitality at every pore'. Any severe rift in the skin of the double and consequent heavy leakage of vital energy affects the tone of the whole vital body much as severe bleeding affects the physical body.

We do not know whether the skin of the double always breaks down when disturbance exists in deep-seated organs, but a bad break in this skin itself can upset deeper seated tissues by throwing the local organization awry, and organic disturbance often registers at the skin level as hyper- or hypo-tension or in other ways, frequently causing leakage as a secondary condition.

The functions of the double in regard to health are very complicated and will be considered after other aspects of the vital body have been described.

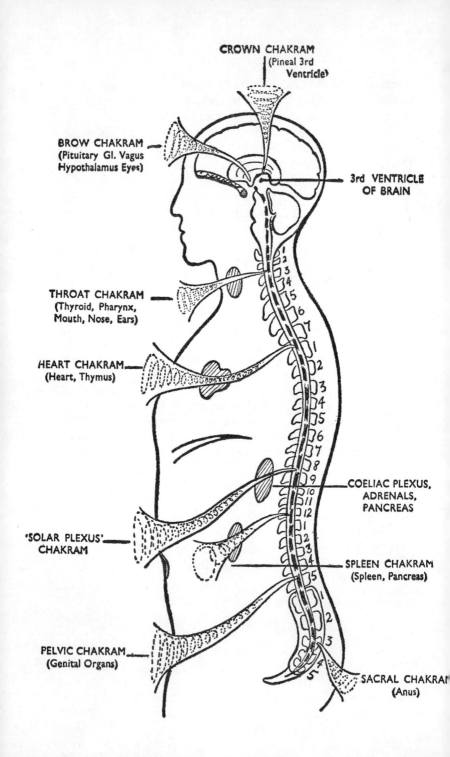

CROWN CHAKRAM
(Pineal 3rd
Ventricle)

BROW CHAKRAM
(Pituitary Gl. Vagus
Hypothalamus Eyes)

3rd VENTRICLE
OF BRAIN

THROAT CHAKRAM
(Thyroid, Pharynx,
Mouth, Nose, Ears)

HEART CHAKRAM
(Heart, Thymus)

COELIAC PLEXUS,
ADRENALS,
PANCREAS

'SOLAR PLEXUS'
CHAKRAM

SPLEEN CHAKRAM
(Spleen, Pancreas)

PELVIC CHAKRAM
(Genital Organs)

SACRAL CHAKRAM
(Anus)

CHAKRAS AND RELATED MATERIAL

Chakram	Region Influenced	Glands Affected	Approx. Spinal Contact
Crown	——	Pineal	——
Brow	Basal ganglia, mid- and hind-brain	Pituitary	1st Cervical
Throat	Throat Base of nose UpperThorax Hands, Arms	Thyroid	3rd Cervical
Heart	Thorax	Thymus	8th Cervical
Solar Plexus*	Upper abdominal cavity	Adrenals	8th Thoracic
Spleen	Left Side of Abdomen	Spleen Pancreas	1st Lumbar
Sacral	Pelvis and Spine	Gonads and Pituitary	Base of Spine

* C. W. Leadbeater describes also a chakram about the navel. This is probably active before birth, but when the child is born the balance of activity is changed and this chakram becomes largely dormant. Further facts and correspondences will be found in the charts given in his book *The Chakras*.

THE CHAKRAS AND THE CIRCULATION OF PRĀNA. The most evident structures in the vital body are the chakras.[12] These can be perceived as swirls upon its surface by even partially trained clairvoyants; magnetic healers frequently learn to localize them by touch. They have been described both by competent modern clairvoyants and in the traditional literature of yoga, where they have a special significance. The descriptions vary according to the view-point of the observer and the depth of his experience. Some of the descriptions are symbolic and philosophical and have no relation to the appearance of the structures at the vital level. We shall deal with them here only as they affect health.

The chakras are flower or bell-shaped vortices lying with their edges on the surface of the etheric double. Incoming and outward-going prānas form in each case a double vortex, woven into an intricate and characteristic pattern of colour and number in the petals of each chakram.

The size, delicacy and vigour of the chakras vary with the type of individual and with the control of mind and body that he has achieved. The more self-aware and self-directed a human being becomes, the more he draws his life from his inner consciousness and ceases to react automatically to outside stimuli, the more the life of the chakras develops. They are the subtle organs by which thought and feeling, first registered in the emotional and mental bodies, act directly upon the physical body.

There are seven major chakras in the human body, and a great many subsidiary ones. Students should not be surprised to hear clairvoyants describing chakras in parts of the body not indicated by the orthodox charts, since these are often fully developed and for one reason or another attract attention. We shall deal with the major chakras only.

The seven usually given are those at the base of the spine, in the solar plexus region, over the spleen, over the heart, in front of the throat, between the eyebrows, and over the top of the head. Ancient Hindu books usually mention one at the umbilicus instead of the one at the spleen. It has been suggested that there is a shift of emphasis in the vital currents, a change of function, taking place in the Indo-European races at the present time, due to certain recognized changes in human nature, that is indicated by the difference between the umbilical chakram, a centre reacting to instinctual and animal vitality, and the spleen chakram, the vitality in the latter being related to the action of the lungs and the individual's own breathing rhythm.

The action of the chakras is specialized. This means that each chakram reacts to and draws into the body a special current of vital energy from the environment and from non-physical levels of consciousness. The spleen chakram has as its function that of drawing in the free prāna of the physical atmosphere which, as has been said, is composed of vitality globules. The structure, breaking up and distribution of these have been carefully described by others and the descriptions need not be repeated here. The vital energy of these particles is discharged along the nervous system, flowing through the fatty sheaths of the nerves, not through their fibres,[13] and is distributed to all parts of the body: surplus and devitalized particles then flow out through the pores of the skin and the hair-like tubes described previously. For physical health the intake of physical prāna and discharge of used materials is of immense importance.

Although this prāna is not drawn in through the lungs the intake is directly associated with breathing. The breathing rhythm determines the activity of the spleen chakram, drawing a current of vitality globules through it into the body, and giving to the stream of prānic life the tone or peculiar quality of its own rhythm at the moment. If this rhythm is good, vitality, which has now become a specialized and personal nervous energy, flashes through the whole vital body with something like the velocity of light. The actual breath in the lungs meanwhile does its own work as physiologists have described. It is the breathing rhythm, and the tide of vital energy that coincides with the breath, that affects the circulation of vitality. Deep rhythmic breathing draws in a larger quantity of physical prāna than shallow or irregular breathing. The supply of prāna is greater in direct light and better still in natural or artificial sunlight, but deep regular breathing *anywhere* increases intake and steadies the flow of physical vitality along the nerves. A few steady breaths affect the whole vital body, and continued easy deep breathing can change the appearance of the entire vital aura for the time being, deepening its opalescent colour, strengthening the emanations, raising them if drooping from fatigue, and generally brightening and toning up the body. Thus the supply of prāna in the body is directly related to breathing capacity and to ability to sustain a good average rhythmic breath.

As has been stated, circulation of vitality takes place mainly along the sheaths of the nerves, but every organ, tissue and fluid receives a supply, including the blood stream, the lymph and all glandular secretions.

THE SUBTLER PRĀNAS AND THE ENDOCRINE GLANDS. We have described the spleen chakram as the focus for the intake of physical prāna or vitality. When we come to consider what the other chakras give to the body, we touch upon a subject so foreign to western modes of thought that both experience and very deep study are needed to envisage adequately the concepts involved.

The psychologist to-day recognizes the proven influence of mind upon body, and orthodox research is being made in regard to allied conditions of body and mind. 'Associated mental states' is the term given to psychological conditions which appear in connection with certain physical disorders. It is possible, for instance, to speak of an anxiety heart or of eczema due to emotional hypertension, while the association of duodenal ulcer with worry is well established. How does the mind affect health?

X is afraid and feels sick. The neurologist will explain the mechanism by which certain reflexes produce this phenomenon. But why does fear set these reflexes in action? It is admitted that the solar plexus is associated with the physical expression of emotion and reacts to emotional stimuli through long established instinctive habit, but the mechanism has not yet been described. If emotion were generated in the solar plexus and were purely physical in nature we could perhaps understand, but emotion can sweep upon us from outside, can be worked up and thrust upon us by violent and excited people until the dullest and most resistant nervous system responds.

In the eastern literature on this subject the chakras are considered to be the special organs, developed in the course of evolution, which relate the influences of the subtler non-physical worlds to physical organisms. It is through them that emotional and mental conditions are able to register accurately and immediately upon the physical nervous system.

They are present in the plant kingdom. Psychic and vital vortices exist around growing plants, and life from invisible worlds playing through these induces added sensitivity in plant tissues. In certain more highly developed plants a type of cell evolves in connection with these vortices that is the first sign of a nerve fibre in organic life. Such cells develop by an inductive process. The stimulus of the psychic vortex, primitive as it is, takes place in the invisible worlds surrounding the plant. The increased activity of the vortex induces increased responsiveness in the vital counterpart of the plant, and so the stimulus is stepped down until it impinges upon the physical cells and induces changes in them. Similar vortices are present in animals closely linking their psychic bodies to their nervous systems.

While the mental body is developing in the higher animals and its various force-centres (chakras) are becoming active at their own mental level, mental stimuli play through these into the vital bodies of the animals and so into the physical nervous systems of the evolving animal form. This play of mental stimulus through the chakras is the urge behind the growth of the cerebro-spinal system, just as emotional growth and the organisation of the force-centres at the emotional level assists and evokes the delicate mechanism of the autonomic nervous system. The subtler bodies set the pace for the physical; in biological terms, the function precedes the organ. The process of refinement and increase of response to non-physical impacts continues at the present time and is part of racial evolution to-day.

Thus in man the chakras are vital organs already specialized for the purpose of linking his non-physical consciousness with its physical means of expression. As the average person only knows himself 'to be alive' in his waking, physical brain-consciousness, it follows that the only awareness the ordinary person has in regard to his chakras comes when they upset him—when his throat tightens with self-consciousness or his 'stomach turns over'—a most expressive phrase, describing a sudden reversal of movement in the solar plexus chakram.

Each of the main chakras acts as a channel for a specialized influence from one or another of the psychological centres. This means that they convey to the physical nerves specific influences originating or registering powerfully in the subtler levels of consciousness, both emotional and mental.

The whole emotional nature tends, particularly when undisciplined, to register in the solar plexus chakram. Thought and emotion linked together register in the heart chakram; the higher mental faculties, vision, perceptivity, insight and creative analysis, affect the eyebrow centre; while the throat reflects the inter-weaving of the spiritual man, the I, with his temporary vestures, the attempts of the individual, successful or frustrated, to express something of his real Self to others. The chakram at the top of the head is not very active except in highly developed people, though it will sometimes become prematurely sensitive in psychics, neurotics and hypersensitives, or may be abnormally disturbed by hypnotism, alcohol, narcotics, and anaesthetics. It is a focus for self-conscious choice of a high order, for the creative will, or true volition.

The centre at the base of the spine is almost dormant in the ordinary person. It may be stimulated by special occult training or, in the normal course of evolution, aroused further as life begins to be lived creatively. Abnormally, it can be excited by certain undesirable magical practices, or even by excessive sexuality. The latter impulses, the sexual, are directly connected with another centre, often given as the second chakram: this is not included in the seven mentioned here (see note on page 41). For the purposes of the race the sexual impulses are creative, not merely possessive or pleasurable. When they are used creatively, and when the higher mental and other subtle creative powers are developed, there is a mutual stimulation between the sacral centre and the centres in the head. Structurally there is said to be a connection at the vital level between the top of the head and the base of the spine linking the subtle and the grosser, i.e. denser, creative activities. Such a connecting link is probably not yet known to western physiologists as dissection after death does not disclose it; presumably it is purely vital in character.

The stimulation of creative artistic natures into activity through sexual excitement has often been noticed. Such sexual stimulus is not essential, for some creative artists work without it and even find it incompatible with their work, but the connection between these two forces exists, and derangement of one of the creative centres frequently induces distress in the other, just as stimulus of one will often excite the other.

The major chakras appear to be connected both physically and psychologically with three structures: a segment of the spinal cord, ganglia of the autonomic system, and the endocrine glands. These physical relationships are as shown in the chart.

In practice it has been observed that the condition of a chakram, viewed clairvoyantly or diagnosed by touch, has a definite influence upon the endocrine glands lying within the sphere of its vital influence, and the alterations in psychological states which affect certain chakras alter the action of the allied glands. It is the chakram that alters first, the bodily condition developing frequently much later, after long strain has been imposed upon it by malfunction at the vital level. It is not, therefore, the glands that ultimately determine character, but character that lies behind the ordinary action of the glands. Gland extracts can and do alter the metabolism of the body at the purely physical level, and often restore a nervous equilibrium which enables an unstable psyche to behave more normally; but repeated doses of glandular preparations, as many physicians now realize, rarely continue to have good results.

Both glands and chakras sometimes respond to suggestion. It is possible to give the needed stimulus to the physical organ by direct treatment of the etheric—that is by radiotherapy, exercise, external applications, massage, colour, light or magnetic healing (q.v.)—and if meanwhile the patient is induced to alter his emotional or mental outlook a permament cure or great improvement may result. Deep-seated psychological difficulties which have played upon the nerves and tissues until actual tissue-change has taken place, such as is found in many cases of glandular malfunction, cannot be dealt with easily unless one has full co-operation from the patient. If this can be secured the response to simple direct treatment at the vital level will be in direct relation to the patient's psychological readjustment.

THE FUNCTION OF THE DOUBLE. With this general view of the whole vital structure in mind, together with the indications given in regard to the influence of the psyche upon the chakras, it is possible now to attempt a description of the very complex activities that take place in the etheric double, the relatively static vital structure

surrounding and penetrating each organ and tissue of
the physical frame.

The function of this double is to act as the meeting
point between the activities taking place in the physical
cell, the blood, the lymph, etc., and the complex vital
forces which overshadow and influence metabolism. This
is a new concept to the western mind, and a quite new and
non-mechanical picture of the body has to be built up to
grasp its implications and to understand what really takes
place.

Let us envisage an active, healthy vital organism
surrounding and interpenetrating a vigorous human body.
It pulses with rhythmic activity, and has that quality of
resilience which is so characteristic of fundamentally
good health. The emanations stand out clearly and the
chakras revolve each in tune with the others. This
particular individual is happy, and mind and emotion
are sending steady integrating energy from their own
levels into the corresponding chakras, there to blend with
physical vitality and to sweep through the body, pleasantly
affecting all its activities.

This individual becomes hungry. Food and water are
taken in at the mouth, more or less charged with vital
energies, according to type and preparation. The vitality
globules taken in through the spleen chakram, and all the
subtle forces entering through the chakras, stimulate the
glandular secretions, and otherwise aid in the breaking-
down process called digestion. As assimilation takes
place, the natural salts and the basic elements, carbon,
hydrogen, oxygen, nitrogen, etc., find their way in simple
and elaborate compounds to the blood stream. Then,
through normal circulation of the blood, but partly
pumped along by prāna, or the energy streaming over
the nerve sheaths or inherent in the tiny particles themselves, the molecules of food are at last spread through
the cells of some particular tissue that needs refreshment.
This process needs all that modern science can tell us
about hormones and enzymes to fill in the picture. Each

chakram has its associated endocrine messengers as well as its prānic life, and the two are closely interrelated. Each needs the presence of the other to explain its full effect and the speed and delicacy with which it acts.

At the point where actual protoplasmic change is about to take place within the cells, the double fulfils its function as the matrix within which cell-change and cell-growth can occur. The double, as has been said, constitutes a sheath or closed magnetic field, bounded by tense skin, in which vitality is held in touch with cell contents, and which stabilizes and integrates the localized vital life. The double of a cell has also the still more delicate function of holding the life forces together while their physical form is undergoing alteration. For there is a moment when even the tiny particles of the chemical constituents of the blood stream and of the cell itself break down into still finer particles,[14] fatigue inducing such a break up of the cell protoplasm, and bodily heat and the right alkalinity of the blood inducing the same change in the contents of the blood plasma. At this point the vital forces dominate, the etheric double holding suspended but active the true pattern, or archiblasts, of that particular cell tissue, and the psychological and physiological forces bringing healthy or unhealthy, cleansing or clogging, integrating or disintegrating influences to bear upon the reorganization of the protoplasm. At each stage the sheath of the double acts as a mould,[15] tending to produce the repetition of that which existed previously, because of all the subtle vital influences which are constantly playing upon and through the double. Sometimes the mould held in the double is better than that suggested by the psychological prānas and their endocrine influences. Sometimes the latter are healthier than the present mould of the double. For better or for worse the drama of cell formation is wrought out under these combined influences at the vital level. The psychical and the physical, the inner and the outer, the influences tending towards change and those which hold fast to habit, meet and mingle in the double. When each tiny drama comes to its culmination the protoplasm formed is minutely better or worse than its predecessor, and the organ deteriorates, or improves, or continues as before, according to the main trend of the forces involved.

Scientific comparisons will suggest themselves. Crystals precipitate cleanly under the right conditions, in confusion and disorder if foreign matter or other disturbing influences are present. The closest comparison is probably that of a grub changing into the larval state and thence into an insect. It has a definite shape as grub or caterpillar, weaves its cocoon and then quite literally disintegrates into a milky fluid: only the archiblasts remain. From this total collapse of form a completely new shape emerges, with differently formed body and legs, often winged, and altogether different in habit of life and in capacities from the grub.

It is here suggested that the double is just such a cocoon, the stable mould in which protoplasmic granules in their most minute form—the 'countless lives' mentioned by Madame Blavatsky[16]—themselves break down into a formless vital mass, possibly into that which has at times and under certain conditions been called ectoplasm. Out of this intermediate condition the granules again reshape themselves according to the long-standing habit of the body, expressed in the double, but continually influenced by those conscious and unconscious psychological forces that play through the chakras and glands and their hormone messengers.

Waste products are then eliminated in two directions. The chemical waste which has perhaps never been broken up into finer forms is drawn off by the usual physiological channels, or remains to poison the tissues. Unused or partly used particles, the waste products at the vital level, may be discharged directly through the vital emanations, or may be swept on by the flow of nervous energy, by the blood stream or by currents of prāna, of which there are many, until it is likewise discharged through an orifice, a chakram or the skin of the double.

The tendency of the double as a whole to secure its own healthy continuance needs to be given great weight. It will seize on any vital material to make good a deficiency and will reinforce weakness in one place by drawing strength from another. This concept of the self-preserving proclivity of the double in general, and of its component parts in their own areas, may shed light upon certain current psycho-physical problems. Many research workers to-day are investigating the possible existence of an influence working at the biological level to which the term 'an organizer' has been given. The evidence for the existence of such an organizer would appear to us to be evidence for the activity of the double acting as matrix for local cell tissues in a complex organism, as well as for each living entity as a unit. We should consider the double in this capacity as a purely physical phenomenon.

In the long run, however, the higher prānas, those emanating from the emotional, mental and other levels are stronger than the double. Worry will disturb the whole structure, insecurity will weaken cell building in given areas, while a calm mind and equable emotions will enable the bodily automatisms to make good repairs and eliminate useless waste with the most unpromising materials. The healthy vital body pictured above would be able to make good cell plasm out of sardines, hot buns and strawberry jam, and the body would sleep well after it!

If this description of the activities of the vital body is well founded, it presents at least a satisfactory working hypothesis as to the mechanism by which mind affects health. The double is the stable matrix for cell growth and tissue change, and the psychological influences, working through the chakras, the nervous systems, the glands, and all their associated vital energies, affect each cell at the moment of growth or resolution through their influence upon the double. Eastern tradition and practice maintain this to be the case, and recent experiment is now providing corroboration.

THE FOUR VITAL TYPES. All that has been written up to this point applies to the vital body in general. We must now consider certain variations in the quality of the vital body, variations which fall roughly into four main types, each with a characteristic flexibility or rigidity, fineness or toughness, heaviness or lightness, both of texture and of material. As the nature of the vital body is determined not only by what is ingested but also by the psychology of the individual influencing the subtle prānas, it will be clear that these four types are characteristic of certain temperaments, but it is purely as physical (vital) structures that they will be described at this point.

We should like to emphasize the fact that the classification below was arrived at in the first instance entirely empirically, as the result of clinical observations of vital bodies made by workers over a period of some years. When the group arrived at a need for classification, experience was pooled, the four vital types now given below were roughly outlined, and some of their characteristic diseases noted. Later it was realized that these types probably had a direct relationship to the classical temperaments of Galen, Paracelsus, Jung, and others.[17] Further research will be necessary to ascertain the physical and psychological characteristics associated with the ancient classifications and to relate these satisfactorily to modern equivalents.

We have termed the four types (1) the heavy, (2) the fluid, (3) the nervously active and (4) the bland. The basis of classification may in the long run be found to be that of the predominance in each body of material corresponding to one of the four classic elements, earth, water, fire and air as used in classical and astrological tradition. In the human being these four types will ultimately no doubt be related to the predominance of various endocrine patterns. For the moment we must use our terms just as symbols, not yet clearly defined or fully understood.

There are no pure types. The types constantly overlap, as each person has something of all four elements in him, though one usually predominates.

The Heavy or Earthy Type. In appearance this is dense, closely packed to the physical form, the chakras stocky. People with such bodies have great vitality, but vary in regard to stamina. Patients of this type are unusually suggestible when emotionally friendly, but are otherwise resistant and frequently prejudiced and rigid. They are normally vagotonic and tend to suffer from muscular overstrains, including myocardial trouble, and from organic congestions such as rheumatism, appendicitis, etc. They generally need treatments which relieve congestion, these giving release to pent up energy.

The Fluid Type is usually associated with people who have strong but over-receptive emotions. Somewhat heavy etheric materials predominate in the vital body, but such individuals are over-active emotionally and this keeps the chakras whirling or sagging with consequent instability in the whole vital structure. People with bodies of this type are often mediumistic and interested in healing work but tend to pick up the patient's condition and to become ill themselves. They may have very good mental ability and when controlled are intuitive and creative. Characteristic diseases are digestive troubles and those associated with bad circulation and nervous inco-ordination. They have vague moving pains and recover unaccountably. The autonomic nervous system predominates over the cerebro-spinal. The best forms of treatment are those that stabilize and calm.

The Nervously Active or Fiery Type is found in very intelligent, mentally over-active persons, who tend to worry and yet have unexpected reserves of nervous vitality. The vital body is inclined to be tense and brittle, with a thin rapid flow of prāna. The chakras are normally well-shaped and responsive, but inclined to be stretched and rigid from overstrain, and are therefore over-active. Such people have as characteristic diseases neuritis, migraine (also common in the fluidic type from directly opposite causes) and cerebro-spinal disorders. The central nervous system is dominant and the most beneficial treatments are those which induce relaxation of tension.

The Bland or Airy Type is not common. Natures which build this form of vital body are intellectual and emotionally sensitive and take life rather philosophically. The vital body appears to be rather open-meshed and can be strong yet rather static or inchoate and weak. Exhaustion, diabetes, and disorders of the lymphatic glandular system are characteristic. Quiet is important. The balance of health is delicate and is best left to the patient's own understanding as far as may be possible.

A fifth typical condition may occur as a modification of any one of the four types described above. It arises as a result of definite training along lines of self-discipline and self-awareness, directed to spiritual ends. The vital structure then becomes finer, more responsive, with the higher chakras active and their functions clearly defined. The subtler prānas influence health very directly in such cases, and disease conditions are due mainly to nervous overstrain, to psychological growth or change taking place at a pace to which the physical body cannot adjust itself, or at times to retreats and failures after a period of effort. Patients with this type of vital body tend to give exaggerated reactions to drugs and treatments, and at the physical level simple and mild treatments are best. By no means all hypersensitives are of this type; unless well integrated they are more often of the fluid type.

THE MENTAL-EMOTIONAL NATURE. GENERAL COMMENT ON EMOTIONAL AND MENTAL MATERIAL. Students of occultism and those who follow the Hindu tradition in medicine make a distinction between emotional and intellectual conditions which is not yet established in western thought or practice. In the West we speak of an unbalanced mentality when a patient suffers from severe fits of depression or violent temper, the terms *mental* and *mind* being used to cover all subjective conditions even when these are primarily emotional in tone. Those who accept the basis of eastern psychology not only distinguish between the dense physical body and its vital counterpart but also make a similar distinction between emotional and mental states.

Although the mind and the emotions are functionally interdependent, investigation on psychic lines confirms the traditional eastern teaching that thought and feeling have each their own characteristic quality, or—as the West would phrase it—work upon different wavelengths. The subtle material in which intellectual reactions register is of a finer and more active quality than that in which emotional states occur. If one may use the phraseology of electro-magnetic phenomena, the release of the energy we term intellectual takes place from a subtler level of the material of which the psychic world is comprised, and so is both more delicate and more powerful than those we term emotional. Emotional radiations have a somewhat fluid and watery quality, with a characteristic pulse or two-way movement of expansion and contraction.[18] Intellectual reactions on the other hand are compared with fire, and in modern times with electricity. The constant use of intellectual and emotional wave-lengths by an individual, and the appropriation of the subtle images formed by thinking and feeling, in terms of 'my feelings' and 'my ideas' builds around each person a definite form or body, the psychic or mental-emotional field of personal experience. To the trained psychic such bodies, of animals as well as of human beings, are distinct and characteristic in the same way as the physical body is characteristic of each individual.

Eastern psychology has always taught the substantial nature of thought, and there is in principle no scientific reason for denying this. On the contrary it gives a convenient language for discussing phenomena outside the

reach of scientific observation and, even if not literally
true, has the sanction of being pragmatic.

The comparison of thought and feeling to electricity
and magnetism, given in the introduction, is convenient
and should be held in mind. The ordinary man or woman
of the world is unaware of any difference between thought
and feeling, since he has rarely, if ever, consciously
experienced them apart from one another. Yet careful
self-analysis will make clear the fact that they are actually
different in nature and quality, and behave differently.
If by analogy we consider thought as representing the
structure of an object—i.e. that complex of energy-waves
which makes what we look upon as solid matter—then
feeling represents that other kind of vibration which we
know as colour. All material objects have both form and
colour, the two being inseparable. So it is with the psychic
or mental-emotional body. Yet *in principle*, structure can
be considered as one thing, colour as quite a different one.

THE MENTAL-EMOTIONAL BODY, OR PSYCHIC AURA. The
following is an account of clairvoyant observation of
the mental-emotional aspect of man, the psyche of the
psychologist. It is couched in terms of the substantial
nature of mental and emotional 'material' and of the real
existence of the psychic body in space-time.

The clairvoyant describes this part of man's nature as
an ovoid, extending some one and a half to two feet
beyond the physical form. It thus also includes within itself the space filled by the vital body. It is full of rapidly
moving colour and of more or less transient forms, the
colour being chiefly generated by feeling, the forms by
thought. Each colour is said to be associated with a
different quality of feeling; the forms are directly related
to the object thought about. They may be concrete, such
as the picture of a house or a tree, or an abstract repre-
sentation of some principle, or a mathematical sum. In
the latter case they are diagrammatic in character, merely
symbolizing the matter under consideration. When
mental activity is heavily influenced by emotional feeling,

the forms in the psychic aura tend to be indefinite, but washed in vivid colour. When on the contrary, the activity is chiefly intellectual, and of an objective character, the colour is subordinate to clear cut form. There are of course all grades of combinations, from a formless torrent of colour in violent passion to the coldest and most geometric patterns of logical or philosophic thought.

THE EMOTIONAL NATURE. GENERAL. Certain schools of modern psychology regard libido, or the force of desire, as the activating principle of the human personality. For somewhat parallel but even more fundamental reasons, emotion is viewed by the occult student as the life-force of the personal nature. The density of the medium in which it acts lies between that of mental and physical matter, and in behaviour it links intellect to body, binding them to each other in a threefold strand—a symbol often used in eastern literature. It is the nature of emotion to ebb and flow, to have a dual reaction. This ebb and flow has been analysed and tabulated by eastern psychologists and is beginning in the West to be noted as the peculiar characteristic of emotion.[19]

Ancient philosophers as well as modern research students have observed the polarization of emotional experience into pairs of opposites between which the personal consciousness swings back and forth. Thus love and hate, attraction and aversion, pleasure and pain, like and dislike, in relation to the same object, can exist at the same time in a given personality, with first one phase and then another dominant. The term ambivalence is used for this condition in modern psychological literature; and emotional ambivalence, or two-way feeling towards one or another object, is usual in most human beings.

The blood, with its rhythmic beat imposed by the action of the heart, provides sound analogy. In eastern terminology the blood is said to correspond at the physical level to emotion, and very quickly reflects emotional conditions. (See list of correspondences, p. 121.) Moreover, just as the blood is the life-carrying stream which feeds both nerve and muscle, so emotion is recognized as the normal vitalizing force of both physical and mental activity, and freedom of emotional life automatically brings vigour to both mind and body.

THE CHAKRAS. Psychic centres exist in the psychic body as in the etheric and are localized at the same points over the physical frame. They have approximately the same shape as those in the etheric body, but are slightly larger and extend beyond the etheric chakras. The complicated nature of these psychic organisms, which link the inner life of man to his physical body thus begins to be evident.

The relation of these chakras, their development in different types, and the stage at which they become consciously controlled by an awakened intelligence and hence fully operative, are all matters for future research.[20] All that we know at this moment is that emotional moods, both conscious and unconscious, do definitely affect centres in the psychic body which are localized and which act as psychic organs for the transmission of influences from the world of thought and feeling into special areas in the physical body.

Eastern physiology and psychology have always acknowledged the direct relation of the emotional life to the 'fires of the body', or physical vigour. Modern research has recently revealed the relation of emotion to the release of endocrine secretions. While we accept much of what is written on orthodox lines concerning the effect of sudden feeling, fear, excitement, desire, upon the important functions stimulated by the sympathetic nervous system, we nevertheless envisage emotion as psychic activity which does not necessarily depend for its inception on intellectual or on physical sensory stimulation, however closely it may be associated with bodily or mental states. It has developed in the past in association with physical stimuli, and has been further stimulated and reinforced by thought-pictures, but it can and does act independently of both, as, for example, in the sudden psychic fright of animals, children and hyper-sensitives, upon whom panic descends for no reason; or when the influence of a given place is calming or other-wise, entirely apart from, and often in contradiction to, its outward appearance. In such cases, fright or excite-ment, acting at the emotional level, sets material swirling, and this intensified activity is instantly reflected in the corresponding vital chakram and through this affects the sympathetic nervous system and the endocrine glands. In lower animal forms, where the instinctual life is dominant, this is seen in its purest form. The occult student places the chief focus of instinctual activity at the mental-emotional level, so his teaching on this point is entirely consistent. Once the cycle of instinctual activity has been established it can be stimulated from the physical or mental level as well as from the emotional.

Other chakras affect the appropriate vital centres very strongly at times when special feelings irritate, block or stimulate their action, but the solar plexus chakram always remains the normal centre for registering emotion, feeling and passion, as distinct both from sentiment and from purely mental activity.

The determining influence of the sympathetic nervous system upon all the fluids of the body, upon circulation of the blood, digestive secretions, etc., is well known. In occult literature the emotions are said to correspond to, and hence to have a hidden influence upon, all fluids in the body and not upon the blood alone, while the mind directly affects the nerves and nervous energy, or prāna.

Inhibited conditions of emotion, however, frequently affect the vagus nerve indirectly, 'pulling upon it', as clairvoyants describe it, through a distorted solar plexus chakram and consequent distortion of vital balance in the area of the solar ganglion. The vagus is also affected indirectly by an overstimulation of the sympathetic reactions, for as these become exhausted, a vagotonic condition is left dominant. Thus very emotional people may have either a plus-reaction of the sympathetic system or a plus-reaction of the vagus, each condition developing either directly or as a secondary condition from overstrain of the complementary function.

For example, the following general and opposite conditions have been observed in intensely emotional people:

A. Persons with a dominant sympathetic system, chiefly emotional in outlook, usually with little mental control, though sometimes with a dramatic imagination.

Nervous system: sympathicotonic.

They give direct solar plexus reactions: solar plexus chakram is often splayed out and reacts violently to shocks, etc. They can be sick easily and get well immediately afterwards. In such types the sacral plexus frequently tends to congestion, and menstrual difficulties follow. They sometimes fall about and may be clumsy and self-conscious. They are frequently greedy about food.

B. Primary vagotonic types, very emotional but more intelligent, and critical in mental attitude.

Here the solar plexus chakram tends to be cramped, tight and hard, the spleen chakram tends to cramp also, and the vital body becomes easily congested and inactive, hence weakened. They are liable to liver trouble and gall bladder congestion, and are often irritable. They frequently suffer from intense overstrain and even migraine.

For psychological and even for physical treatment it is important to recognize primary and secondary reactions in the above conditions, i.e. primary emotional stimulation may bring about sympathicotonia but be followed by exhaustion of the sympathetic nervous system which may reverse the condition in the physical body. This means that at a given time in sympathicotonic types the vagus may predominate, contracting the heart muscles, etc., because the exhaustion of the sympathetic system has occurred through overstrain. The converse is also true.

EMOTIONAL STATES AND HEALTH. The emotional material interpenetrates the physical and vital bodies and by a form of inductive action frequently produces vague generalized sensations or actual change in vital conditions. The emotional life does not feed the physical body directly, but it stimulates the vital circulation by its own flow and by increasing healthy activities in the chakras. It is an interesting psycho-physical fact that health can be obtained at almost any moment, no matter what the circumstances are, if enough emotional energy can be freely released to sustain in this way the immediate activities of the physical frame.

A person with an impoverished emotional life lacks energy at the vital level. To have vigorous health it is necessary to adjust oneself to the environment in such a way that emotional life is released and may flow freely. This is frequently a difficult task, and much of modern psychological literature is a study of this need. Activities which are largely unconscious tend to be instinctive and automatically repetitive. Much so-called human thought and feeling is repetitive, like a gramophone record, which plays from start to finish once a suitable stimulus has set the thing moving. To clairvoyant sight these repetitive patterns and habitual moods lie in their own areas of the psychic body as inert masses of material of a given colour and quality, and any associated stimulus will wake one of these masses and start it into active motion, so that it spreads out over the whole aura, obliterating other less active material and, for the moment, dominating the whole field. The waking brain of the individual affected is usually unable to fathom what has happened. If such a condition is acute the person is 'overwhelmed' with feeling, quite literally, but unable to define or direct his state, because it lies beyond the range of his present conscious control. Clairvoyants can see this happen as a visual and objective experience, as one would watch a stormcloud gather in the sky.

Old influences brought over from the past are sometimes extremely important factors in starting up such a train of reaction. These seeds of potentialities brought over from the past experience are in the aura at birth, hence a certain automatism of the subtler aura is already established. We do not come into life with a perfectly clean sheet, but with certain tendencies already inherent. Environment calls these out more or less quickly and strongly. Mental and emotional tendencies brought from past lives are much more automatic, convulsive and irresistible than those built by present circumstances. They may be said to lie a layer deeper down than the ordinary complex of thought and feeling, which is concerned with this life's problems only. Technically they may be said to be the protopathic material out of which the epicritic complex is built.

The health in many people depends upon the free flow of emotional life. When the emotions are healthy they are able to perform their work of interplay with, and stimulus to, the mental, the vital and the dense physical bodies.

As man is a social being this means an adequate adjustment of his nature to his environment.[21] Here one may compare Groddeck's theory of the methods used by the unconscious to obtain a state of equilibrium between the psyche and its circumstances.[22] In the attempt to attain this balance compensation plays an obvious part, and compensative reactions need to be carefully studied in the case of many patients. There is the instinctive, fantastic, child or worker who day-dreams, and is often anaemic because so much energy is dissipated unproductively in the psychic field. He allows emotional life to leak away at its own level and is frequently very much dissociated. Then there are those who must objectivize their compensations by boasting and lying. The Adlerian school of psychology has good reason for its emphasis on social adaptation as the most satisfactory basis for helping these and other types to equilibrate themselves. Social values tend to check and correct over-compensation and unhealthy fantasy. If a condition of comparative equilibrium between the individual and his environment can be established the flow of emotion will be adequate for health.

The practitioner is probably perfectly familiar with the effect on health of the following:

(a) New interests, marriage, travel.
(b) Frustration, inferiority, conflict.
(c) Shock, and the variability in recovery when the patient is happy, or unhappy, and also when the shock is purely physical, or has some deeper emotional implication.

Equilibrium is of various kinds. It may arise from harmony within oneself, independent of environment, or more usually from some mutual adjustment that harmonizes the personality to its circumstances. Thus a satisfactory sexual life may bring physical harmony, and the creative moment of art may do the same.

Deep poise, or established equilibrium at the emotional level itself, is usually due to adjustments made by the individual at a much deeper level of his consciousness. It is always characterized by a sense of effortlessness and of adequacy to meet life. Such poise gives a clear focus to the whole consciousness, for when the emotional nature is calm the mind can act with lucidity. It also permits a deliberate control of health from the interior levels, working outward to the physical body. Only an individual who is integrated and whose personal nature is self-directed can sustain this. He may be a very simple person, but he has the knack of being aware of himself at any given moment. Such simplicity is not that of the cabbage state: it is wholly conscious. The effect of conscious integration upon the emotional nature is that of clarifying and stilling it, so that the current of the emotional life may become a sustained and outflowing stream.

While this condition is not likely to be arrived at by the ordinary patient, a physician or healer may glimpse it in himself as a consummation towards which he may sincerely labour. The true healer gives the impression of being a fountain of some interior energy. A calm outward-turned quality of the emotional nature permits certain subtle forces from deeper layers of human consciousness to well up freely.

THE INTELLECTUAL NATURE. GENERAL COMMENT. In the analogy referred to earlier in this chapter, mental and emotional activities were compared to electricity and magnetism, which are always found together and yet work under known, distinguishable laws. In abnormal states of dissociation there may be a split between mind and emotion, and trained minds can learn to operate with conscious detachment from emotional conditions, but usually the two are found working together.

It has already been pointed out that emotional activities have a characteristic quality of duality, an ebb and flow, noted as ambivalence in modern western psychology but given a very fundamental significance in eastern literature. In this literature the desire nature of man is said to oscillate between the pairs of opposites throughout his whole cycle of evolution. Only by the development of Self-awareness, and the discrimination that results from this, can an individual free himself from the confusion and psychological distress which is caused by the recurrent shifting of his personal feelings from one pole to the other. The emotions, as we have noted, make their physiological impact upon the autonomic nervous system, and this reflects the dualism of emotion in its twofold activities of stimulation and retardation of metabolism.

Intellectual activity, on the other hand, does not ebb and flow in this fashion. The mind may be either sluggish or over-active, but unless strongly influenced by emotion its attitude over a given period tends to be fairly constant.

The physiological reaction of mental activity is upon the cerebro-spinal system and affects chakras that play directly upon the brain and the whole of the spinal cord. Emotional disorders only affect the brain indirectly, through toxemia, exhaustion, shock, or strain upon the vagus nerve. By bearing these wide correspondences in mind a key to the deeper roots of physiological disease is sometimes available. Correspondences will be considered more fully in the chapter on diagnosis.

In the thought-world the objectivity of psychological conditions and reactions is more defined than at the emotional level. Emotion washes back and forth in waves of colour; thought works in lines and surfaces. It builds objective structures which a well-trained mind can maintain for relatively long periods of time. Thought in eastern literature is considered to be the capacity for establishing relationships,[23] and weaving patterns, that is arranging ideas in relation to each other, is the characteristic habit of an active mental body. These patterns are at least three-dimensional, in so far as our concept of dimensions applies to the subtle intricacy of mental matter. Only as the thinker is able to reproduce in his own mental body a fairly true image of the subject under consideration does he comprehend it clearly. The image may be slight or complete, distorted or accurate: the quality of the image built will indicate the extent or limitation of his understanding.

The mind-world, like the emotional, exists in itself, and human mental bodies are that part of the general mental material which each person has appropriated and used as his own. Being composed of mental matter they are readily influenced by the activities of the mind-world—i.e. of what C. G. Jung calls the collective mind—around them. 'Pressure of ideas,' 'currents of thought,' etc., are objective conditions at that level, and the human mental body is astonishingly open to influences from the thoughts of other mental bodies in its neighbourhood. In therapy the thought-influences thrown around a patient, for better or for worse, have more to do with his nervous conditions and mental attitude than most physicians are prepared to admit.

Because of the ease with which mental material takes

on and holds a shape, each individual has a well-defined mental area which he uses as the field of his personal mind. This appears roughly as an ovoid form. Personal thinking consists in building up within this ovoid forms or images associated with the subject under consideration. The clarity, completeness and exactitude of the forms produced depends upon the mental habits and abilities of the thinker, on lines familiar to ordinary psychologists. The mechanism of thinking (and particularly of remembering) depends upon the ability of the mind to create forms related to the object thought of. When full attention is being given to an idea or an object, its mental counterpart may fill the whole of the mental ovoid. Such a large pattern will later shrink and fade away entirely if the attention given to it has been merely transient. If, on the other hand, the idea is recurrent, then when attention is withdrawn and emotional interest in it dies down, it will lie in the aura as a tiny seed-thought. When stimulus of some sort again stirs this group of associated ideas into activity, the whole pattern expands and may again fill the ovoid.

The Gestalt school of psychology, working on a purely physiological basis, has shown how such 'wholes' are closed in upon themselves and act as a unit. To clairvoyant sight the springing into activity of such a 'whole' is like the expansion of Japanese 'magic' flowers when placed in water: the colour, the shape and texture of the idea, plus a charge of emotional feeling, assert themselves complete. This is perhaps the most usual form of thought formation and behaviour in the ordinary mental body.

There are other forms of thinking which the Gestalt theory, in our view, does not cover, but as they are not essential to our subject they will not be described here. Actual mental disorder will be dealt with under 'Morbid Mental Conditions' (page 82 *et seq*).

All the behaviour patterns of the mind are subject to the epicritic faculties of the highest consciousness, the

Self. Through the development of latent discriminative and self-critical faculties a human being is able to break up automatic and conditioned formations in his own mental structure. When so freed, the mind-body becomes able to reflect both external and subjective experience realistically and with lucidity.

THE CHAKRAS. The chakras at the mental level are located in the same areas as in the other bodies. The petals and mouths of each lie on the surface of the mental body, the stalk running back and enclosing the stalks of the emotional and vital centres, so that mental, emotional and etheric forces interweave in each chakram.

MENTAL TYPES. One of the characteristics of the mental world is a fairly clear division between its dense and its subtler levels. In these descriptions the terms 'higher' and 'lower' mental fabric, or matter, may occur. Although this follows the theosophical nomenclature, Professor Francis Aveling[24] and others have recognized the qualitative difference between repetitive, conditioned mental activity, and insight, or creative thinking. Concrete or lower mental activities take place in slower and heavier mental matter than do the higher. In this heavier material are found the forms built by concrete thought about objective matters, and these are relatively dull in colour and heavy in structure. Creative thinking, whether artistic, philanthropic, or an act of creative perception, is clearer and more beautiful in colour and lighter in texture. The mental bodies of different types of people vary enormously in the relative amount of the lower or higher mental material which they habitually use. Some quite clear thinkers rarely contact subtle mental life at all. The ovoids of their mental bodies are filled with concrete thought-forms about matters of fact and everyday sensory experience. At the other end of the scale there are mental ovoids which are so filled with abstract or higher mental material that it is difficult for the individual thinker to form a clear-cut picture of physical plane objects. He lacks the necessary apperceptive mass, as the psychologist would say. The eastern student would say that he was unaccustomed to using the particular type of mental material required to build that type of thought, and so was unable to build the appropriate mental form with any degree of accuracy.

FUNCTIONAL RELATIONSHIP OF THE VARIOUS LEVELS. The task of the physician, the true healer, is to evoke in the patient the desire and the ability to establish real health in himself as far as possible. To do this in cases of chronic disease it is necessary that some degree of balance should be restored at each level—metabolic, prānic, emotional, mental—in order that the activities of the patient's various aspects of consciousness may be co-ordinated to each other. With undeveloped types, as has been said, this can frequently be done by change in diet or régime, by change of interest, a sea voyage, etc. An outside stimulus strong enough to bring even a temporary unity to such a patient's consciousness will permit the body to function harmoniously for a period and so may bring a return to health. With deeper-seated difficulties and more self-critical natures, the patient has usually to understand what changes are necessary and to some extent to take upon himself the responsibility for making them.

SELF-DIRECTION AND HEALTH. We have not yet considered the relation of the spiritual man to his psychic and physical equipment. This has been in the past the peculiar field of religion rather than of science, but the East does not divide these two aspects of experience as does the West, and has therefore developed a technique of self-direction from the level of the spiritual consciousness which, though founded on religious tradition, has been continually tested by renewed and exacting experiment. This technique is called yoga, a term referring to the releasing of the life of the individual from its automatic and instinctual bondages, its personal habits, so that it is freed to reorientate itself to the One Life, the underlying substratum of existence. There are many forms of yoga. Some of these, which demonstrate the control of the psyche over physical function, are now receiving serious consideration from western psycho-therapists.[25] The religious aspects of this subject do not concern us here, but only the fact of the power of the inner nature to influence the personal bodies by sub-ordinating each in turn to its own dominant influence.

Experiments in India and France[25] have demonstrated, through the use of the electrocardiogram, that a *genuine* Indian yogi can control not only his breathing and pulse but also the action of the heart muscles. In a series of records taken while a yogi was entering deep trance the breathing graph flattened out first, then, after a struggle, that of the pulse, and finally that of the heart muscle itself. The man in this condition was, by this type of scientific evidence, moribund. At a given signal the yogi returned to his body, and the graph became normal. Experiments by Dr. Brosse and others in France with the same instrument demonstrated the immediate reaction of the heart and pulse, etc., to variations in mental and emotional conditions.

The above facts, and others of like nature, are steadily accumulating, and are forcing western medico-psycho-logists to appreciate the need for a scientific approach to the problem of self-direction in thought and feeling, as well as in physical hygiene. We cannot here discuss the problem of which methods are likely to prove effective for different temperaments. A suggestive reading list is appended.[26]

In our opinion it has been very clearly demonstrated that the central, or inner, consciousness in man, function-ing at a deeper level than thought, can select, direct and cultivate, without repression, those mental attitudes and feelings that conduce to health and happiness and that release energy freely at all levels.

The effect of such co-ordination from within outwards is to bring to bear upon the personal nature a new type of energy, entirely unlimited and self-sustaining. The picturesque terminology of eastern literature describes this condition as living directly 'upon air and fire instead of upon earth and water'. The extraordinary feats of eastern students of yoga, when genuine, are made possible by the release of this type of energy, directed by a trained will and co-ordinated intelligence.

We do not envisage the production of any such phenomena as being part of the doctor's work, but we do see the possibility of reversing the usual attitude of mind and of training the personal consciousness to look not to external aids—such as medicine, physical treatments or a series of specialists—for its ultimate health, but rather to a re-organization, a re-education, of its modes of expression, so that these can be infused and sustained by inner vitality. The personal bodies can thus become more and more harmonized through the growing control of the Self, and the continuing health of the physical body is assured by a deliberate alignment of all the levels of consciousness from within outwards.

Ill health may occur, and probably will, at periods of great stress, and especially at times when the individual is pushing his self-awareness through into still subtler levels of hitherto automatic behaviour. But such illnesses can be met and cured as the psyche yields itself increasingly to the direction of the Self, the spiritual man. Health that results from the use of reasonable physical treatment combined with a quiet determination to achieve further psychological freedom is both resilient and sustained.

In the new outlook on medicine which is developing to-day the psyche and its activities are taking a recognized and important place. We suggest that the distinction between thought and feeling, as outlined above, is important, and that a study of the varying influences which they bring to bear upon the nervous systems and the general metabolism of the body will be part of the emerging science of healthy living. If the influence of the inner man, the Self, can also be included in such a study the goal of therapeutic treatment will indeed be seen to be *mens sana in corpore sano*.

No.	Page	
1	29	Francis Aveling: *Personality and the Will*, p. 87. Cambridge University Press.
2	30	See Appendix: Reading list on Hindu Medical Science.
3	30	The Government Indian Medical School Hospital, Madras.
4	32	Crile, in *The Phenomena of Life*, with his concept of the radiogen, seems to be getting near to the eastern teaching.
5	32	J. E. R. McDonagh: *The Nature of Disease*, 3 Vols. Heinemann.

G. W. Crile: *The Phenomena of Life*. Heinemann.

A. D. Speransky: *The Basis for the Theory of Medicine*. Lawrence & Wishart.

Georges Lakhovsky: *The Secret of Life: Cosmic Rays and Radiations of Living Beings*. Heinemann. A significant contribution to the study of human radiations just issued for the first time in English while this book is in the press.

| 6 | 33 | Shiva is a name of the Divine Being, in its aspects of destroyer and releaser, and, in certain attitudes as creator also. |
| 7 | 33 | E. Jacobson: *Progressive Relaxation*. University of Chicago Press. |

E. Jacobson: *You Must Relax*. McGraw-Hill.

A. P. Call: *Power Through Repose*. Gay & Hancock.

| 8 | 33 | Langdon Brown: *The Sympathetic Nervous System*, p. 13. Hodder & Stoughton, 1923. |

A. Besant: *A Study in Consciousness*, p. 154. Theosophical Publishing House, London, 1915.

A. Gardner: *Theosophical World University Bulletin*, 1931. No. 2, p. 8.

| 9 | 34 | Professor J. E. Marcault, in a lecture delivered to the Theosophical Research Centre in London, January, 1938, referred to the research work being done in France on the two kinds of electrical activity in the human body. In this connection he has supplied the following references. |

P. Mollaret: *Interprétation du Fonctionnement du Système Nerveux par la Notion de Subordination*. Masson & Cie., 120 Boulevard St. Germain, Paris.

A. L. Tchijevsky: *Les Phénomènes Electrodynamiques dans le Sang*. Editions Hippocrate, to be obtained from Le François, 91 Boulevard St. Germain, Paris.

| 10 | 35 | P. Payne: *Man's Latent Powers*, p. 44. Faber & Faber. |

W. J. Kilner: *The Human Atmosphere*. Kegan Paul & Trench.

A. Gardner: *Vital Magnetic Healing*, Theosophical Research Centre.

No.	Page	
11	37	O. Bagnall: *Origin and Properties of the Human Aura*. Kegan Paul & Trench. W. J. Kilner: Op. cit., Chap. IV.
12	42	Singular 'chakram': plural often given in English as 'chakrams'. C. W. Leadbeater: *The Chakras*. Theosophical Publishing House, Madras, India. P. Payne: *Man's Latent Powers*, pp. 48-60. Faber & Faber. P. Payne and L. J. Bendit: *The Psychic Sense*. Faber & Faber. G. Hodson: *The Science of Seership*, pp. 58 and 209-216. Rider.
13	43	Cf. A. V. Hill: 'Nature of the Nerve Impulse', *Nature*, April 8th, 1933. Also references given under 12.
14	50	Possibly Ether 4 or Ether 3. See Smith, Slater and Reilly: *The Field of Occult Chemistry*, Chaps. I. and II. Theosophical Research Centre.
15	50	'Protoplasm has the potentiality of remembering something about stimuli which have been sent into it, and of releasing such stimuli in various degrees without the aid of all the original stimuli. This is virtually what is understood by Habit-Formation. It becomes engraved on the ultimate particles of cell-protoplasm.' C. J. Patten: *The Memory Factor in Biology*, p. 73. Baillière, Tindall & Cox, 1926.
16	51	H. P. Blavatsky: *Secret Doctrine*, Vol. I, pp. 269, 281. Theosophical Publishing House, London, 3rd Edition.
17	53	I. Geikie Cobb: *Glands of Destiny*, pp. 9-14. Heinemann, 1927. C. G. Jung: *Psychological Types*. Kegan Paul.
18	56	Bhagavan Das: *The Science of the Emotions*, pp. 21-25. Theosophical Publishing House, Madras, India, 1924.
19	58	A. Besant: *A Study in Consciousness*, Chap. XI. Theosophical Publishing House, London.
20	59	P. Payne: *Man's Latent Powers*, pp. 17, 32, 33, etc. Faber & Faber. See also *The Psychic Sense*—ref. note 12 *supra*.
21	63	J. Drever: *An Introduction to the Psychology of Education*, pp. 59, 60. Arnold.
22	63	G. Groddeck: *The Unknown Self*, Chaps. I, II, III. Daniel.
23	66	For full discussion of colour, etc., see C. W. Leadbeater: *Thought Forms*, and *Man Visible and Invisible*. Theosophical Publishing House, London.
24	68	Francis Aveling: *Psychology: The Changing Outlook*, pp. 51-52. Watts.
25	70	T. Brosse *Bulletin du Centre Homéopathique de France et de ses Filiales*, p. 187. Feb. 1937. See also Ref. 9 above.
26	70	See Appendix: Reading list on Directed Thinking.

Chapter IV

ETIOLOGY AND PATHOLOGY

Morbid Conditions

G ENERAL REMARKS. In the usual medical textbooks diseases are treated under specific groups according to their presumed causation. These groups include diseases caused by bacteria, those caused by physical agents, the intoxications, and diseases of metabolism and deficiency. Following such a classification, the different parts of the body and their peculiar diseases are considered: under each disease its etiology is discussed, together with its morbid anatomy, pathogenesis, bacteriology and bio-chemistry. The result, to the student, is a splitting up of the problem of disease causation into complicated details, for to each minutely different deterioration of function or of tissue a different name is given and different experimental treatments applied. Hence the student has to deal with a maze of detail very difficult to co-ordinate or assimilate effectively.

There is, however, a fundamental cause underlying all diseases, which has been somewhat overlooked by the orthodox workers of the past generation. It is the condition of the soil, or field, in which disease develops: in other words, the general condition and tone of the body, the host. There are for instance bodily conditions in which certain bacteria can live innocuously, doing certain useful work. A change occurs and they become morbid and develop pathological qualities. In the latter case the bacteria become associated with certain deteriorations of function and tissue to which the names of special diseases are given. The importance of the field in relation to the development of bacteria is only gradually being acknowledged in the teaching of medical schools, but certain research students consider it to be the determining factor in the metamorphosis of bacterial forms. Mr. J. E. R. McDonagh has published a monumental work upon this subject,[1] while Speransky[2] in Russia emphasized the significance of the condition of the nervous system as a factor which determines resistance to disease.

As this basic factor comes to the fore the new approach to medicine will almost certainly tend to simplify both method and terminology.

Mr. McDonagh's position is that reaction to infection on the part of cells depends upon the condition of the electrical field within which metabolism takes place, and he has developed a technique for restoring a healthy balance to this field by the injection of certain chemicals. Its results, however, are not sufficiently conclusive to command general acceptance.

Many disease conditions, however, yield satisfactorily, and without after-reaction, to modern methods of diet, relaxation of nerve tension, osteopathic adjustment, ray therapy, or, if more deeply seated, to psychotherapy, rather than to injections or to specific medicines. The effect of such generalized treatments is, apparently, to increase the normal resistance of the body to infection, i.e. to restore the normal balance of the interior electrical field.

The recognition of the existence of the vital body provides an explanation for the success of such general treatments, since they tend to restore a ready flow of prāna; and the flow of prāna, or nervous energy, is the chief determining factor for the bio-electric conditions within a living form. Whereas the relation of drugs to the stimulation or release of nervous activities throughout the body will always remain a subject of major importance to the medical student, the recognition of the existence and functions of the vital body, and of causes of disease other than physical, will certainly tend to simplification of technique at the physical level and so avoid elaboration of detail as well as of terminology. The emphasis upon the study of variation in the manifestations of disease conditions may very well give place to that upon ways and means of restoring general physical tone, and thereby allowing the body to produce its own antidote.

Lack of tone, of health, of resistance to infection, at the physical level is, in our view, directly connected with the behaviour and condition of the vital and mental-emotional bodies. As this opens a new range for the study of human pathology we shall proceed at once to give a description of certain pathological conditions in the vital and subtler bodies. Needless to say, the greater part of the information given is the result of clairvoyant investigation or was obtained by other methods of extra-sensory perception. A very fruitful source of knowledge concerning abnormalities in the vital body was the work of a group of masseuses and physio-therapists, several of whom developed an extended sense of touch for diagnosis and treatment.

Morbid conditions in the vital and subtler bodies exist concurrently with disease conditions in the physical body. We should like to emphasize the fact that disordered function and even deterioration of characteristic structure in the vital and other bodies have been observed *before* any corresponding disturbance became manifest in the physical body. Hence in the study of hygiene and of preventive medicine the recognition of the existence and behaviour of the subtler bodies assumes very great significance.

MORBID CONDITIONS IN THE VITAL BODY.[3] The outline that follows concerns the disorders of the vital body in general and applies, with inevitable modifications, to all four of the vital types.

The chief of these disorders may be grouped under five headings: (I) fatigue; (II) distortion; (III) congestion; (IV) depletion; (V) collapse. These characteristics can be distinguished from each other because, in extreme instances, they are clearly defined. In practice they will often be found to occur simultaneously in the same individual. Yet the distinct conditions do exist, and will be considered in outline form for the sake of clarity.

(I) ORDINARY FATIGUE. The causes and physical symptoms are the same as for ordinary physiological fatigue. To clairvoyant sight or touch the double is either contracted or loosened a little, according to type, and the emanations droop or wilt slightly, the flow of prāna being lessened. Sometimes the emanations tend to thicken and become short. Ordinary rest and standard treatment for fatigue restore them to normal and they recover as wilted flowers recover in water, gradually raising themselves to their usual position. Quiet, easy and slightly deeper breathing hastens this process perceptibly.

(II) DISTORTION. This occurs when any of the currents which form the vital structure cross, bend or become tangled. Examples: a thickened or tangled mesh of vital material over a wound; a kink in the stalk of a chakram. Distortion is nearly always present; even in fatigue the emanations often fall together and become slightly tangled.

(a) *General distortion.* There are vague and diffused distortions when the vital structure is neither congested nor depleted but just lacking in alignment. *Causes:* varied —emotional shock (purely physical shock leads to collapse rather than distortion); too great general excitement, as in over-stimulated children; conditions of unrest and confusion. Physical symptoms are certain types of pain, vomiting, sudden fatigues, faulty metabolism, vague physical distress.

(b) *Distortion of chakras. Causes:* The distortion of a chakram is a special state always due to sudden or chronic psychological conditions such as fear, anger, retreat from contacts, acute egotism, etc. Shock, both physical and psychological, can make a chakram contract convulsively, and the chakram's return to normal activity will depend not only upon correct treatment at the time but also upon the patient's psychological background and the habitual behaviour of the chakras. For example, a healthy-minded child or adult will recover from an accident or operation in a few weeks, the chakras involved becoming quite normal in that time, but a patient who has been habitually anxious or fearful beforehand may develop a permanent kink in the head or solar plexus chakram as a result of shock + anaesthetic + unchanged habit. Any strained psychological attitude, either 'good' or 'bad', registers in the chakras, as we have said, the distortion-creating element being the fixity or tension of the psyche, independent of motive. Thus a child striving too hard to pass examinations, through pride or fear, or an idealist over-working because he 'cannot do enough' to help his fellows, may each develop chakram strain.

Physical symptoms are those of pain or cramp along the line of the stalk of the chakram, malfunction of organs and glands lying in the area influenced, or the typical disease conditions and metabolic disturbances associated with the glands influenced by the chakram that is distorted. If more than one chakram is affected a general weakness and lack of recuperative power is often present. Frequently, distortion of a chakram is the cause of depletion or congestion in the vital body as a whole (III and IV below), but it may also be due in part to one of these factors. The symptoms and causes of such inter-related states will be dealt with under the next headings.

(III) CONGESTION. This term is used to describe the condition which arises when for any reason vitality does not flow normally from the orifices and surfaces of the body, but silts up around organs, joints and special areas. The whole body can be congested, the flow of prāna being generally inhibited or sluggish; or special areas may be affected, as in a sprained wrist or in constipation. *Causes:* (a) Physical: (1) structural blocks, such as an 'osteopathic lesion' or a strained muscle; (2) toxic conditions due to bad food or water, constipation, drug residues from too much medicine, and septic foci. (b) Psychological: strained, fixed and unwholesome mental and emotional states register as distortions in the chakras, and the check or disturbance in the flow of prāna in the area influenced by the given chakram results in local congestion. Psychological conditions may also work directly upon the tissues, without the mediation of a chakram. Examples: incapacity to express oneself may block the throat chakram, and congestive throat trouble may develop; a too intense sense of responsibility may lead to congested conditions in the shoulders or nape of the neck. The psychological states causing such difficulties may be roughly generalized as those which check, store up or withhold energy, e.g. resentment, possessiveness, retreat, inferiority without compensating outlets, active self-interest, etc. Diffused congestion can also arise from similar but less definite causes.

Distortions arising from congestion are like those arising in a blocked tube. Prāna, used and unused, piles up behind and around the block and the double becomes murky with accumulated material. The radiations then thicken or bend and the flow in them is sluggish.

In a congested area the organs are affected or not according to the patient's type and also according to the whole system of correspondences between mind and body (see page 121).

Physiological effects are usually those associated with auto-intoxication, constipation, catarrhal conditions, congestive headaches, and sometimes with an apparent lack of energy although the body in itself is vigorous.

(IV) DEPLETION. *Causes:* (a) Physical: (1) structural block, as before, the depletion arising *beyond* the block, as in anaemia of the brain due to a lesion between the atlas and the skull or axis. The flow of prāna is inhibited by the congested conditions of the tissues around the atlas, and the head can be starved for want of prāna just as much as from a reduced blood supply. In such circumstances, the emanations beyond the block droop and wilt and the double loses resilience. Such depletion can arise beyond any block formed by congested structural or etheric conditions. (2) Actual muscle or nerve exhaustion from excessive physical activity or malnutrition. This depletes the double. (3) Drugging, from many medicines of a sedative or stimulative nature; also exhaustion of the vital body from too great a variety of treatments given to the physical body. (b) Psychological: again, disturbance of the chakras can cause depletion of the vital forces, as when the chakras are stretched or splayed outwards from avidity, complulsive activity, excitability, etc. Prāna is then driven through the vital body with great intensity, stretching and depleting the double as an overheated iron scorches and impoverishes a cloth.

Physiological effects are those associated with anaemia, nervous exhaustion, mucous membrane fatigue with catarrh as a secondary condition, neuritis, etc.

(V) COLLAPSE. At times the life of the vital body apparently ceases to function, and the radiations fall together in a tangled mass or sink in upon themselves, shutting up like a sea anemone half withdrawn. This very extreme condition we have termed collapse. *Causes:* (a) Physical: shock of any kind, extreme toxaemia, nervous exhaustion. (Extremes of III a.2. and IV a.2.) Anaesthesia: the vital body is driven out in part by anaesthetics and sometimes does not flow back correctly. Repeated anaesthetics, particularly at short intervals, can produce distortion of the vital body and even collapse. Certain drugs in excess, alcoholism, etc., can produce a real dislocation or a rift in the vital body. (b) Psychological: to produce collapse in the vital body, psychological disturbance is almost always combined with over-activity of the dense physical nervous system. Psychic shocks and psychological hypertension, extreme dissociated states, panic and melancholia can then play upon chakras and nerves until the vital structure sags and collapses.

Physiological effects: extreme physical exhaustion is usual: the patient faints easily, goes into deep, unrefreshing sleep, or cannot sleep at all and suffers from panic. Vague or acute moving pains are frequently present.

ACUTE DISORDER OF THE VITAL BODY. In acute diseases the appearance of the vital body alters considerably. Congestive conditions, such as inflammation, acute toxaemia, fibroid and malignant growths, are accompanied by accumulation and congestion of etheric matter in the locality (see III above). Portions of the body not yet affected may remain fairly healthy but the congestion favours infection, when fever may develop. Fever thins and distends the vital body,[4] while subsequent exhaustion leaves it limp and depleted.

UNUSUAL VITAL CONDITIONS. Nothing has been said about conditions due to misuse of psychic power, or to sexual excesses, nor about the damage caused by ignorant use of yogic breathing exercises, nor of other abnormalities of the vital structure, of which, unfortunately, not a few instances exist to-day. They are too intricate to be discussed here with any real usefulness. They can frequently be improved by common sense and such methods as those mentioned below.

The foregoing is a very brief summary of diseased conditions in the vital body. Fortunately, the old-fashioned remedies of the intuitive practitioner act as much on the vital as on the dense physical body. Such remedies include rest; correct diet; deep breathing; sea-bathing; and the time-worn but excellent remedy of 'a change', which evokes new currents of vitality and allows distortions to relax and ease themselves. Then there are the more modern treatments with light (in moderation), and colour, and the too-little recognized treatment by vital magnetic healing;[5] these affect the vital body at its own level and frequently restore it to health.

Direct psychological treatment, when successful, releases the basic pressure upon the chakras by easing out mental and emotional fixations and changing psychological habits. It may fail, however, in certain cases where the physical difficulty is subtle and of long standing, because both psychologist and patient lack knowledge of the conditions present in the vital body, which may well need special treatment to enable it to respond to a new influx of life.

MORBID CONDITIONS IN THE PSYCHE. A detailed study of disturbance of mind and feeling has, in the past, belonged to psychiatry rather than to general medicine. For our part we agree with the medical psychologists who feel it to be of paramount importance that disorders of the psyche should be correlated with those of the physical organism. Hence, although a discussion of the deeper aspects of psychic disorder cannot be included, a brief description will be given of characteristic mental and emotional disturbances found in the ordinary patient. As in the descriptions given of conditions in the vital body, these are also based upon direct observation of many cases over a period of years. They are in no sense traditional or authoritative.

The mental-emotional body, or psychic aura, registers accurately every form of psychological disturbance. These appear to the clairvoyant in different ways. A person of rigid mental patterns has a corresponding stiffness in the aura. A flexible mind has a quickly moving aura. In the rigid mind repetitive or persistent thoughts create certain fixed images which either stay unmoving like a picture from a magic lantern, or repeat themselves in short sequences like the pictures in an old-fashioned zoetrope. In anxiety states the fear causes a shrinking away from the object of fear. If the anxiety be fear of life in general, the whole aura remains tight and cramped. Such conditions can easily become habitual and inhibit the free flow of psychic energy. This naturally reacts on the vital body and eventually causes trouble in the dense physical.

In general, persons with strong emotional surges of feeling tend to suffer from congestion, confusion, and irregular movement of psychic material, whereas the characteristic disordered states of more rational types are those of rigidity, over-activity, and a tendency to split off or shut off portions of the psyche from the whole. These tendencies are doubtless due to the inherent differences in the qualities of mental and emotional material, i.e. to the fluidity of matter at the emotional level, and to the far more fixed and separable qualities of the mental substance used in ordinary thinking.

In the emotional sphere congestion may be due to excessive love of excitement and undue stimulation, or, more usually, to accumulation of emotional material unused through lack of outlet. The emotional nature then sags or becomes like a writhing mist, and is very much inflated. Confusional emotional states, due to ambivalence or to conflict of some sort, have every conceivable form of manifestation at their own level, associated with characteristic functional diseases in the physical body. The physical conditions vary according to individual characteristics. For example, a conflict between personal devotion to a friend and personal attachment to interesting work would register differently in one who was heavily emotional as compared with a more intellectual individual. If the feeling nature dominated, the solar plexus chakram would tend to pick up the emotional backwash and probably disturb the digestion, even bringing on sickness; whereas a more mentally active nature might register the conflict through a congested brow chakram resulting in recurrent headaches.

In the mental structure, rigidity can be due to fear, egotism, and other similar states. In this condition the mental body may be either thin and brittle or turgid and congested, but it has no resilience. Stupid people with suppressed emotions can develop this state, as well as clever people with fixed ideas. Over-activity in the mental body may be due to mental avidity, ambition, fear, to an undue or forced withdrawal from emotional to mental activity, or to any of many other very common causes. When the mind is over-stimulated by the deflection into its field of suppressed emotional energy, the mental material whirls and spins with terrific activity, and often wears out the vital sheaths of brain and cerebro-spinal

nerve tissues, upon which it reacts directly at the physical
level.

General withdrawal from life tends to produce a shell-
like carapace into which nothing can penetrate and out of
which nothing can come. On the other hand the over-
stimulated, excitable person, boiling with more or less
suppressed curiosity and avidity for experience, has an
aura that whirls and spins in all directions creating the
whirlwind atmosphere which either fascinates or repels
other people so that the individual person concerned
becomes 'the life and soul of the party' or else 'that
dreadful person'.

Thus it is clear that psychological states produce
comparable states in the aura which are frequently
sensed if not seen by the average run of people, who
express them in such colloquial terms as 'green with
envy', 'feeling blue', 'exploding with anger', 'drenched
with self-pity', 'wet' and so on.

The tendency of the mental body to split bits off is
enhanced by the fact mentioned previously, that thinking
is done on the Gestalt principle, i.e. in localized wholes
which tend to rise to conscious awareness all in one piece
and to drop again into the background of thought without falling apart. If such wholes become more and more
aloof from ordinary thinking, and from contacts with
physical reality which challenge their validity, they may
become systematized within themselves and form a
delusion. A person perfectly sensible concerning ninety-
five per cent of his affairs can be completely irrational,
indeed insane, about the other five per cent. Eccentricity,
extreme prejudice and other fixed habits, usually with a
great deal of emotion attached, belong to this type of
mental maladjustment which, in serious cases, is labelled
as paranoid. The amount of life flowing into such a closed
mental system and the degree of feeling attached is
evident to psychic perception, for they appear as actual,
visible structures at the mental-emotional levels, small or
large, dominant or latent, literally 'all-absorbing' or

negligible, according to their development. As detachment of mental processes from the general life of the mental body sometimes affects physical health adversely, more details will be given. There is always emotional energy associated with these detached mental processes, often a great deal. The mental fabric holds the thought-pattern steady: emotion adds vigour and enhanced interest.

There are three main variations in the relation of these particular psychic morbidities to physical health. (1) In this the fixed mental state is only a small part of the mental body, and it absorbs so little of the total life-force of the individual that the effect upon the whole is negligible and the physical body can remain healthy. Examples: a strong prejudice or a favourite 'castle in Spain'. (2) Here a hidden and often unconscious mental-emotional fixation expresses itself in some form of fixed anxiety about health and so may produce conversion hysteria, the body becoming slightly or seriously affected; or, in another type, the absorption of attention, and consequently of the psychic life-force of the person, assumes undue proportions, and the physical body becomes depleted or 'fades away' because the energy which should be stimulating its activities is short-circuited at an inner level. In this latter condition the life-force of the patient is literally absorbed by the mental-emotional structures, which develop at the expense of the physical body. Examples: hysterical headaches, preventing social contacts; the day-dreamer who becomes tubercular. (3) This is a borderline state, or definitely psychotic. In it the psychic structure is entirely detached from physical contacts of any kind and the patient lives in it as in a world of his own; the physical body is sometimes even exceptionally healthy, eating and sleeping well in a completely undisturbed physical circuit, while the psychic life functions in its own circuit, entirely out of alignment with its vital and physical centres. If a person who has been in this third condition begins to recover normal co-ordination between the mental, emotional and vital centres, developing self-critical capacity or beginning to break up the abnormal mental structure in some way, he may for a time pass through a period of serious physical ill health. This happens because the increased alignment of his bodies now allows the mental disturbance, which has hitherto been present but cut off, to register in the chakras of the vital body, and so to disturb physical functions. The possibility of the appearance of disturbed physical health in the case of a patient who has been suffering from psychological trouble which has been serious, but from which he is recovering, is well known in ordinary psychotherapeutic work, as also is the fact that if the mental adjustment proceeds further the physical disorder may clear away in the usual fashion.

Psychotic states can only be mentioned here. The student should read Henderson & Gillespie's *Textbook of Psychiatry*,[6] in particular, or other orthodox handbooks. The above work is especially referred to because the classification there given follows Kretschmer's and is closely allied to the theosophical analysis of man's constitution. For those to whom this textbook is not immediately available the following outline is appended.

Henderson and Gillespie (re-arranged)	*Comment*
A. Organic reaction types: blood conditions; alcoholism, drugs; gases, etc. febrile; syphilitic; psychoses from brain changes; psychoses from general diseases; metabolic deficiency.	Physical and vital bodies are chief centres of difficulty.
B. Affective reaction types: manic depressive; involutional melancholia.	Emotion dominant, out of control, or screening off the external world. Functional dissociation between thought and feeling.

C. Schizophrenic reaction types.
Mental-emotional body split. Conflict between opposing elements in the psyche, thought and feeling strongly interwoven in each of the opposing elements.

D. Paranoiac and paranoid reaction types.
Connection between spiritual self and personality probably affected: 'delusions due to enhanced expectation', ideas of grandeur, etc.

In both C and D the mental values are cut off from contact with other people's values.

Psychoneuroses, including neurasthenia, anxiety states, hysteria and obsessive compulsion states, are regarded as other than the above, although those suffering from such disorders may belong to any of the above types. Certain forms of epilepsy and mental deficiency are classed by themselves.

A FEW NOTES ON PSYCHOTIC STATES. When psychological difficulty is present in an acute form, i.e. when the patient is actually or nearly psychotic, the condition may, as we have said above, be confined to its own level, or it may have a physical manifestation. In some cases psychotic derangement tends to be externalized through cell changes.

(a) The disorder of the higher principles disorganizes the vital activities and so stirs up a potential and latent disorder, such as syphilis, in general paralysis of the insane.

(b) Hysterical symptoms appear. These can be conversion hysteria, i.e. a transferred effect from a somewhat remote psychic conflict, such as motor paralysis due to a hidden sense of guilt; or direct conditions due to the fixed mental-etheric mould built by the patient's thought, as when a male patient produces labour pains, having a fixed idea that he is pregnant. In our opinion the physical conditions reported by the hysteric are actual, i.e. pain or immobility actually exists, because the vital mould built by thought is present. The effectiveness of suggestion in such cases is due to its attack upon the thought processes which maintain, and a change in which can therefore dissipate, the mould (see under *Suggestion*, page 174).

(c) The patient introduces into the system drugs, narcotics, etc., which bring about dullness of the physical reactions and ultimately affect tissues.

A clairvoyant has contributed the following brief notes on certain reaction types:[7]

The *manic depressive* has a fixed thought-pattern strongly charged with emotion, which lies at the bottom of the aura when quiescent. When roused it stirs into activity at the base of the aura, gradually enlarging its area of disturbance in a sort of spiral until the whole aura is suffused and distorted with it. At its peak of activity, it works in a spinning way right up to the top of the ovoid, reaches a crest of intensity, and then dies down. This is true of panic states, manias, and, to a lesser extent, of any conditions in which there is some sort of fixed recurrent grievance.

The *schizoid* flares out and flickers, oscillates, and is frenzied; is always in a state of acute activity in opposite directions at the same time.

The *paranoid* blows out the mental body with egotistic feeling and walks round in this as in a bubble, cut off from contact with reality.

In borderline conditions or those of actual insanity there is always a break or rift, sometimes very pronounced, in one or more of the subtler bodies. Just as the vital body can develop a leaky spot through fatigue, overstrain or shock, so the mental-emotional body may also be worn thin by excessive worry or mental over-activity, and this will register as a thinning of the aura at a given spot. The thinness increases slowly until it becomes a V-shaped rift. In those actually insane this is usually over the head. If treatment is successful the rift gradually closes up, in good cases from the bottom upwards, like a well-healed wound.

CAUSES OF DISEASE

GENERAL REMARKS. Science to-day takes a far less rigid and dogmatic attitude towards all natural phenomena than it did in the last century. The nineteenth-century mind, accustomed to a strictly departmental arrangement of material, accepted readily the idea of direct or simple causation. So the mentality of the 1850's and onwards accepted without much query the concept of specially-causative germs, each specifically responsible for creating a given disease.

Science to-day tends increasingly to agree with the occultists' view that nature is an organic whole, with closely related activities overlapping each other at every level and on every hand; any one apparent cause is in itself the result of a complex of preceding causes which must be held in mind when estimating any sequence of events. Such an attitude is consistent with the views of those orthodox research workers who more and more recognize that natural phenomena, including those of bio-chemistry and physiology, take place in a complex situation of balanced forces. Even this balance is continually being disturbed by progressive changes, each change establishing a new and temporary equilibrium in the congeries of forces with which it is involved.

In regard to the causes of disease the trend of opinion nowadays is rapidly altering, and the theory of direct causation by specific germs is undergoing considerable modification. Research has proved that many diseases can exist without the presence of a specific germ, and that a particular germ can be present without the inevitable development of the disease.[8] It becomes necessary, then, to recognize that some factor within the patient is also required for the disease to develop in virulent form. While admitting that the presence of certain organisms is one of the conditions which indicate the presence of disease, we must now accustom our minds to thinking in the wider terms of group causation and not look for a simple germ as the ultimate cause, or even for a single theory as an ultimate explanation. As we have seen, the interplay of man's psychic bodies upon each other is as much a factor in health and disease as is the interplay of any one physical body with its immediate environment. The physician who views the patient as a whole has, indeed, to see the problem of his health as a minute reflection of the problem of the whole universe, for each individual is constantly affected by social and even cosmic influences, as well as by his own psyche, by his personal environment and his reactions to it, by his diet, his breathing, and his capacity to rest.

The concept of a given germ as specifically causal for a given disease condition is, however, so deeply established to-day in both the lay and the medical mind that we have thought it advisable to devote special attention to this point before proceeding to consider wider aspects of the subject of disease causation. The following section is a brief summary of some current views of prominent medical writers and research workers upon the relation of germs to disease processes.

THE RELATIONSHIP OF GERMS TO DISEASE.[9] The true relationship between germs, or micro-organisms, and disease processes is one which is neither so simple nor so capable of final proof as is commonly believed by the layman. The teaching of Louis Pasteur, that the germ is the disease and the disease is the germ, is by no means borne out by the evidence of bacteriology; and even the scientific postulates of the germ-theory, originally laid down by Robert Koch, have had to be considerably modified in the light of later knowledge.

As the medical correspondent of *The Times* explained in 1926 in reviewing the annual report of the Medical Research Council, 'When the discoveries of Pasteur became known to the medical profession in this and other countries a very simple idea of the relationship existing between man and his disease was formed. . . . It is now seen that these ideas will require some modification in the light of more recent discovery and there is no more interesting portion of the annual report of the Medical Research Council (1924-1925) . . . than that which sets out the reasons for this change of view.'[10]

The implications of this change were earlier pointed out by *The Lancet* in a leading article as far back as 1909, when, in discussing certain facts for which this theory (the germ theory) does not account, the writer declared that 'the question then naturally arises: are these so-called organisms truly causal, or are they only "secondary invaders"? They may perhaps be normal inhabitants of the body, only assuming importance in disease.' In illustration of this contention *The Lancet* called attention to a paper by Dr. William Hamer, later Sir William Hamer, in which he quoted many instances 'to show that the "causal organism" is not capable by itself of inducing disease and that a *tertium quid* must be assumed'.

It may be remembered that Dr. Hamer, as the result of his study of the investigations of Dr. Houston, Water Examiner to the London Metropolitan Water Board, came to the revolutionary conclusion that as regards typhoid fever the evidence supports the theory 'that it is typhoid fever which leads to the development of the bacillus' and not vice versa, and that 'the bacillus should be looked upon as effect rather than cause'.

This was in 1915, and since that time medical thought has travelled far towards the acceptance of the opinion expressed by Sir Frederick Keble in *The Times* of October 8th, 1935, that 'It was believed that the source of all evil and disease was microbes. At this moment the thrones of the microbes had begun to shake. They were known for what they were, merely the agents or puppets of a weak prime minister—malnutrition.'

There cannot be any doubt that the trend of bacteriological research has been to show that the greatest factor in determining the effect of introducing micro-organisms into the body is the condition of the soil in which they find themselves. A reviewer of *Recent Advances in Disease of Children*[11] wrote: '. . . alterations in the chemistry of the body are antecedent to infection. . . . Deranged metabolism should be regarded as of greater import in the causation of disease, and infection is to be looked upon as an incidental factor imposed upon the metabolic disturbance. . . . The main part of the philosophy of disease must be concerned with changes in structure and in function, rather than with the action of agents which gain access to the body from outside.'[11A]

In fact, in most modern textbooks on bacteriology statements will be found to the effect that bacteria will not of themselves cause disease.[12] Both tetanus and gas-gangrene bacilli are typical instances of organisms which are innocuous if washed before injection.[13]

Dr. Chalmers Watson called attention in *The British Medical Journal*[14] to the fact that 'Bacteria played an important part in the causation of disease, but these were for the most part normally present in the digestive tract, and were, during health, innocuous.'

It is also held upon high authority that diphtheria bacilli, for instance, 'do not live long in a healthy throat',[15] and that even people who have been proved by a chemico-biological test to be susceptible to the specific toxin do not develop diphtheria when infected with the virulent bacilli, so long as their mucous membranes remain healthy.[16] We reach the conclusion, therefore, that it is to the condition of the patient himself, as a whole, and not to any specific microbe that we must look for those factors which are the true causes of disease. This, of course, is only re-emphasizing the ancient teachings of Hippocrates and Galen.[17] The latter laid it down as one of the fundamental conceptions of the origin of disease that '*no cause can become efficient without an aptitude of the body*'. Like Hippocrates, he laid special emphasis upon the importance of *crasis*, or temperament, and habits of life, while ascribing to the third factor, the *katastasis*, which included meteorological, climatic, and other objective conditions, variations in epidemic forms of disease likely to affect the community.

It is at this point that a consideration of two lines of modern investigation may bring these ancient conceptions of disease into direct relation with present-day scientific thought, and make it possible to substantiate them by reference to the modern experimental method.

The first is indicated in the work of Dr. A. J. Kendall, Professor of Research Bacteriology in the North-Western University Medical School, Chicago, by which he showed that bacteria of the type said to cause diphtheria, tetanus, dysentery and cholera, if grown in culture on sugar, instead of in the usual broth derived from meat, do not produce toxins, and so remain innocuous.[18]

The second is confined as yet to the investigations of Mr. J. E. R. McDonagh, who claims to have traced all the bacteria that are to be found in the body in association with infections which arise from within the body to one parent form, of which all others are evolutionary muta-tions. The factors which, he maintains, determine these changes are (a) the basic habit of life (including diet, elimination and so on) and (b) an influence emanating from the sun, stars and nebulae. The emergence of the latter, no doubt startling, conception from the mind of a modern materialistic scientist, is explained by the fact that Mr. McDonagh regards the universe as a single interrelated chemical system in which changes in the constitution of one part are reflected in every other part of that system.[19]

We know that electrical changes in any dispersed system of particles, of which a colloid is a typical example, are disseminated throughout the whole. Mr. McDonagh envisages the possibility that changes in the relationships of a given aggregation of matter in interstellar space will be followed by minute changes in all departments of that grade of matter throughout the universe. Hence, the very atoms and molecules of that type, or grade, of matter will alter slightly wherever they occur. Those, likewise, that constitute the bodies of man will be affected by modifications or reactions occurring in interstellar space. Mr. McDonagh's very thorough investigations of colloidal activities taking place within the human body have no doubt influenced his opinion, and opened the way for so remarkable a suggestion in regard to cosmic influences.

This is, in effect, a modern presentation and defence of the old astrological theories, of which more is bound to be heard later. The physician of the East has always recognized the influence of the planets, and more particularly that of the sun and moon, with their seasons, upon disease conditions and upon the effect of selected remedies. Soon we may learn that dosing with sulphur in the springtime has more in it than the authority of an old wives' tale!

It is possible here merely to indicate the general lines along which these unusual conceptions of Mr. McDonagh have been developed, but perhaps the brief outline given above may assist the student to obtain a more complete conception of the relation between the micro-organisms and the human body and so prepare the way for a more competent treatment of the disease conditions with which they may be found associated. For, as a writer in *The Lancet*[20] confessed in regard to the hitherto accepted view-point, 'It is a remarkable fact, a fact worth close attention, that the discovery of the relationship of bacteria to disease had led to little improvement in control of the common infections.'

It will be seen from the quotations given that many research workers are now emphasizing the importance of influences that affect the 'soil', or conditions in the human body, and that they consider these to be as important as, if not more important than, the nature and behaviour of the germ itself. With this view we should, as we have said earlier, most heartily agree. From the point of view presented in this book the most important causes underlying disease are those that provide a soil in which the pathogenic forms of bacteria flourish. These include personal factors such as habits of life, thought and feeling, since these, as we have shown, by disturbing the vital organism can result in disturbances of the vital-electric field within the body, and hence in unbalanced metabolism, morbid accumulations, and unhealthy tissues. When the 'soil' is free from toxic material, bacteria can live upon it without detriment to the body (see above, concerning diphtheria bacilli in sugar solution). It is the poisoning of the 'soil' through the disturbance of its electrostatic condition, caused by factors such as those just cited, that allows deterioration to take place in the development of bacterial forms, and so gives rise to special disease processes allied to the type of bacteria developed.

We need also to consider those evolutionary changes in bacterial forms co-incident with changes in matter throughout the universe. On Mr. McDonagh's theory, as well as according to many ancient traditional teachings, changes and re-arrangements in material influences in the cosmos can result in the development of corresponding qualities in bacteria, which will affect the varying types of disease chronicled in the history of mankind. Not the least valuable result of applying the foregoing conclusions to the problem is that cyclic changes in the manifestations of what are regarded as identical diseases, such as plague, influenza, etc., which have been noted at different epochs in the history of mankind, and which hitherto have been difficult to understand, become capable of rational explanation.

These conclusions apply whether the disease is a so-called infection from within or an infection from without. The distinction is an artificial one, for while the causes of disease arise in every case from within, infection, that is to say the dissemination of micro-organisms in the blood-stream and tissues of the body, is always from without. The skin surface isolates the body from the matter of the outer environment. The intestinal flora, concerned with what are usually regarded as infections from within, are also, strictly speaking, outside the body, for the alimentary canal is lined by a mucous membrane that isolates its contents from the body as a physical entity. In both cases either injury or disease must destroy the integrity of the insulating surface before entrance of micro-organisms into the system becomes possible. Pasteur himself taught that an intact and healthy body was proof against the invasion of micro-organisms, and it is this very important fact that needs particular emphasis at the present day. Nor must it be forgotten that in their normal habitat, the alimentary tract and the surface of the epidermis, bacteria have important and beneficial functions to play in the way of breaking down chemical substances into simpler consti-tuents, and that they often render poisonous products innocuous in the process.

INFLUENCES TENDING TO THE DEVELOPMENT OF DISEASE CONDITIONS. Having dwelt at some length upon the relation of germs to disease, we will now consider some of the eastern traditional teachings bearing upon the causation of disease, relating these whenever possible to clinical practice and to modern usage.

According to eastern tradition, the idea that the stars influence health is well founded, but western practitioners should not concern themselves too much with this fact unless they are prepared to make a profound and thorough study of medical astrology. If they keep their eyes open, however, experience will prove that certain types of diseases occur in groups. For example, during a given season throats are attacked, three months later gastric complications are frequent. While this is true of many who are ill during the period, certain people, whose birth or progressed horoscopes do not indicate response to the temporary influence, may not be attacked at all, or may suffer during a prevailing epidemic from some illness to which they are personally prone. With the above reservation, it has been noted by those who make a close study of such matters that epidemic diseases and variations occurring in them, as seen most characteristically in influenza, have astrological parallels and explanations.

Further modern evidence can be cited. Homœopaths, who individualize their cases carefully, recognize that certain epidemic diseases, such as the influenza of a given year, demand a certain remedy, whereas the influenza of another year may demand another remedy. Also, special types of individuals respond to certain groups of medicines. Such types can be grouped and studied under their astrological classifications, as well as under the more orthodox classifications such as sallow, florid, heavy-boned, nervous, etc. There is no doubt that certain individual tendencies in regard to health can be discerned in a horoscope by one who has studied this aspect of the birth map. The actual predominance of 'earth, air, fire or water' in the personal horoscope, for instance, may be a helpful indication.

In support of these ancient teachings there is the fact that the effect of invisible influences upon plant growth is being studied in modern research laboratories;[21] and that the phases of the moon apparently influence germination in plant seeds, and the flow of sap.[22]

Mr. McDonagh's work, referred to above, approaches this whole subject from a materialistic standpoint and yet seems to confirm the theory that planetary, lunar and solar influences actually can, and do, modify cell changes at certain periods, both in man and in nature.

Now although the ordinary person is dominated by his stars, the self-aware individual brings out from the deeper levels of his nature, indicated by the centre of the horoscope, i.e. from his own spiritual centre, forces that constantly transcend and modify the influences indicated both by the birth map and by the progressed horoscope. Hence a slight knowledge of this great science is more misleading than helpful and is not to be recommended for the general practitioner.

We repeat that this is a vast subject, undoubtedly studied as a science in ancient days, and probably soon again to be revived as such. The general practitioner needs only to keep an open mind and observe what he can. It will be many years before really useful information can be tabulated and made available for clinical practice.

KARMA: SOCIAL AND PERSONAL. There is a Sanskrit word *karma*, denoting action and its result inevitably bound together. This word is convenient, and will be used here to denote those influences that impinge upon an individual owing to his relationships with his fellows. These influences are karmic, because they are caused by the existence of the relationships themselves and the reactions of the individual to them. If man is considered as an essentially spiritual entity, using a succession of bodies in a series of incarnations on this earth, it is natural that he should be drawn into that race, nation, group and family which is to be the immediate field of his progressive experience. This is his social karma, and the conditions of his birth, whether in a well-fed clean community or in an ill-drained and pest-ridden slum, would theoretically depend on many confused factors of associations, effort, interest and behaviour of himself and his close companions in other lives.[23]

We do not wish to dwell too much on this rather abstruse subject, however interesting its implications may be. Briefly, the social karma of an individual in regard to health includes war and all social catastrophes; epidemics and other diseases due to social neglect of sanitation or to the existence of slums; contacts with soiled money and other magnetically and physically unhealthy objects; prostitution, excessive alcoholism in the community, etc. Group activities, such as clubs, links of business association, political activities, schools, dance halls, etc., all come under this head. These of course affect the potentiality of health, particularly that of children. An adult can usually make a choice, of individual karma, in regard to such factors, though he is not always free to do so; but he can generally be more careful as to what physical contacts he makes.

HEREDITARY KARMA. The eastern student would consider that an hereditary predisposition to a disease, as well as all congenital malformation, would be due to behaviour in past lives. The physician will of course treat all such diseases by the best known methods, but he will find it useful in dealing with certain obscure or deep-rooted conditions to seek out the trend in character that has laid the patient open to his present affliction. Take, for example, epilepsy. Nowadays, this is often recognized as being associated with deeply-resistant and frustrated emotional states, and the patient almost always needs to be educated to accept some limitation of self-expression. Other factors are frequently present, such as deficiency of calcium, but learning to accept frustration without resentment may be the basic point in an epileptic case upon which a good reaction to medical or manipulative treatment will depend. So-called hereditary epilepsy, therefore, is fundamentally an expression of the patient's own psyche, brought over from his own past experiences in other lives. Certain children, born in the same family as those who become epileptic, do not develop this particular disease because they are of a different temperament and so escape it.

The attitude so frequently met with—'all my family have rheumatism'—or the fear of some hereditary taint, should be noted as a factor tending to create the disease feared. It is true, as we have said, that the fact that the individual is born into that family may mean that his personal karma includes here the possibility of his developing the family complaints; yet the viewpoint suggested would encourage the physician to take a very positive attitude towards hereditary trends, and shows that it is possible that these can often be arrested, if not completely overcome. Consider the now old-fashioned fear of hereditary tuberculosis: weak lungs may be a family difficulty, but modern knowledge and facilities can usually prevent the occurrence of tuberculosis itself.

In this connection a point that needs very particular emphasis is the distinction between true heredity, as represented by the handing-on of characteristics through the chromosomes of the parent germ-cells, and the transmission of those intimate personal influences that are brought to bear upon the embryo during the ante- and post-natal periods. The term congenital, as distinct from hereditary, should be used for these latter. It was no doubt with this distinction in mind that H. Oertel used the word 'heredity' when he wrote that 'Diseases are never hereditary; diseases are processes'.[24]

The family attitude is another matter. It frequently happens that a genuine replica of the familial complaint may develop in another individual not only through expectation, but by a psychological indentification with a loved or feared person suffering from a dramatic or painful disease, or through a still more subtle influence which might be termed a psychic contagion. This inner influence, enhanced by similarity of food, living conditions, and identification with the family view-point, is very frequently mistaken for family heredity.

The karma that permits an individual to be born of inferior stock, so that the body is weakened or contaminated from birth, is a very difficult one to meet, but it can be helped by adopting the attitude that since in some life a healthy physical body will have to be achieved, why not in this one? The process of slowly altering negative physical tendencies may take more than one life, but extraordinary rapid results have been obtained in persons who have been induced to give full co-operation and to take both interest in, and responsibility for, the building up of a positive, healthy tone at all levels and in all the bodies.

PERSONAL KARMA. While an individual is always an integral part of the social whole, there are certain aspects of his life over which he has considerable personal control.

His reactions to special situations are due to the condition of his own psyche, and the result, at least in so far as it affects his own health, is personal. Here the reader is referred back to the description[25] of the method by which states of mind, and of emotion, breathing, food, water, etc., are woven within the vital matrix into the continually-rebuilding physical body. The matrix itself is affected by thought and feeling just as much as it is by air, food and water. When an individual selects his own food and makes a choice of what he drinks he determines his own health. His karma in this matter, i.e. the result of his action, may be long delayed if he has a vigorous body and abuses it, or, on the other hand, if he has the long task of building up an already deteriorated frame. In other cases the result of choice may register immediately in a bilious headache, or as a sense of increased well-being. All that has been said in regard to the importance of psychological conditions, and the relation of the subtle bodies to health, applies here. The fact that a given individual at a given moment comes to the right person for really positive treatment is said, according to this theory, to be due to past causes, actions and conditions. On the other hand, people who are not ready to assume responsibility for their own health are likely to fail to benefit from the approach we are suggesting and will prefer palliative methods which save them the trouble of doing anything to help themselves.

The problem of personal responsibility for one's health is not a simple one, as a disease condition is always a syndrome, and its development differs in each type of individual. All the following factors must be included in any given case: food, water, air, sunshine, etheric type, bodily habits, fatigue, sleep, relaxation, psychological trends, stage of development, social relationships, etc.[26] In general, a healthy person is defined[27] as *one whose adjustment to his environment at all levels is suitable to his stage of evolution*. It follows from this that disease may be the result of maladjustment at one or more of many points, with a consequent disturbance of vital and biochemical equilibrium at the physical level. The focus of metabolic disturbance in any given patient will be due to his type and his habits, e.g. anxiety heart will develop in one, gastric ulcer in another, varicose veins in a third, from worry reacting in characteristic ways upon various natures and different vital and psychological types. In a given area, such as the throat, tonsilitis will be a usual difficulty with one person, another will get an encysted thyroid, and a third, vascular thyroid, again according to type. In each of these cases the throat chakram will be disturbed, and that area weakened, by a different condition of maladjustment at psychological levels.[28]

When there is a weakened local condition of the vital structures due to psychological strain, this allows infection to develop in that area. Malfunction may then become chronic, and tissue deterioration take place. The end-result can be organic disease of a serious nature.

Accident. Personal injuries due to so-called accident can often be traced to some psychological cause, such as bad co-ordination, lack of judgment, unconscious retreat from life, etc. Where an individual is, say, riding in a car driven by someone else and suffers concussion in an accident, the karma would either come from past lives or be the result of a psychological crisis, or need, to which the impersonal laws of nature respond in this fashion. A special adaptation to life, needed by the patient at the moment, may be of great assistance in achieving a rapid or complete cure. This may suggest a possible explanation of striking changes of character which sometimes occur as the result of an accident, surgical operation or other severe shock. Much current psychological literature bears on matters such as this.

Infection. Exposure to infection of various kinds is inevitable in modern life, but the karma of becoming infected is individual. The only real protection against infection is that built and maintained by the development of increasingly healthy, flexible and vigorous bodies at all levels. A healthy and positive frame of mind and feeling creates a vital condition resistant to disease, while undue fatigue or bad food, shock, alarm, etc., may at any moment negative an otherwise resistant psychic condition. The positive psychological state induced by having an inoculation against 'flu' may be as important as the dose itself— or even more so, since psychological states react into the vital and dense physical bodies, affecting the soil, or field, in which the bacteria, perhaps already inhaled, are developing. Enthusiastic interest, devotion, and the right kind of determination to carry on, can, through their physiological effects, protect very depleted bodies. Fear diminishes the quantity and speed of flow of the vital forces, and hence diminishes resistance to disease both physically and psychically. A definite or established thought-form of a given disease, such as is so often built in times of epidemic or through nursing a relative or friend through a painful illness, increases the likelihood of infection, as it usually increases fear and helps to establish what might be called the disease wave-length in otherwise healthy bodies. Nurses and doctors, who at times, in their desire to warn the patient of possible danger, dwell too much upon the possibility of serious complications, may very well tacitly suggest their occurrence to an over-sensitive individual.[29]

Psychic Attack and Obsession. Psychic attack is rare as a cause of disease but it does occur. *No obsession by an independent non-physical entity, human or otherwise, can occur unless the door be opened from within by the patient.* The psychic bodies can, however, become shocked or torn by sudden fright, or depleted by alcoholism, drugs, anaesthetics, hypnosis, as well as by wrongly-applied yoga practices, 'sitting for development', automatic writing and other forms of negative psychism. An entity may then adhere to a leaky place in the vital body, provided that the psychological predisposition already exists, i.e. that the patient is already open or responsive to this type of entity. This is, however, extremely rare in

Europe or America, although it is a theory much too often and too glibly put forward by the ill-informed and the psychologically ignorant.

Inexplicable exhaustion, shooting and moving pains, sometimes of acute intensity, are symptoms to note. Certain symptoms, such as hearing voices, a sense of depletion, of weight or attack, can be produced by a dissociated portion of the patient's own personality acting independently. Patients should be discouraged from thinking along these lines, (a) because if the idea is true, thinking about it tends to give the entity a greater hold, and (b) because it is very often used unconsciously as an excuse for bad behaviour: the individual excuses himself by blaming the obsessing entity; and (c) because if the idea persists it needs handling by a well-trained psycho-therapist who has personal knowledge of psychic matters, and should not be treated by an amateur, no matter how well-intentioned.

SUMMARY. As will be seen, the views here presented in regard to the cause of disease deal more with personal predisposition, and with subtle changes in the relation between the patient and his environment, than with determining the exact nature of the tissue deterioration caused by this or that infection.

In the chapters on diagnosis and treatment that follow it will again be found that very little space is given either to infections or to treatments that depend upon the theory that bacteria are the primary causes of disease. With certain obvious exceptions, where specific treatment for certain well-known infections is indicated, we have found that fundamental therapeutic methods such as correction of spinal maladjustment,[30] better diet, correct exercise, sufficient rest, and simple medicaments, combined with adequate psychotherapy, are often more effective in making a patient well than are attempts to cure a difficulty by treating the patient with preparations developed to counteract a specific germ—i.e. symptoms and end-results, not primary causes.

Viewed on a large scale, the causes of disease may be summarised somewhat as follows: Each individual is part of the universe, and is therefore subtly influenced by variations in the macrocosm as well as by those of his immediate environment, such as the people he contacts and their behaviour, the dirt or cleanliness of his surroundings, and the social organization, culture and hygiene of his race, nation and family. But each individual is himself also an organic system, a microcosm, within which resides his spiritual principle, creative, illuminant, healing. It is the behaviour of the individual within the system of his own consciousness that will determine whether in the field of his body bacteria develop beneficently or dangerously, whether morbid metabolic changes will occur, and whether organisms outside that body will invade it successfully or be harmlessly absorbed.[31]

Once an invasion has succeeded or toxic changes have taken place and a disease condition is established, some physical treatment, orthodox or unorthodox, usually becomes necessary; but, even then, it is the patient as a whole who must be healed, i.e. made whole again, if he is to remain well and again become able to resist the inevitable contaminations which surround him in everyday life. The root of disease causation thus lies in the psyche and its reactions to its environment.

> 'Men at some time are masters of their fates:
> The fault, dear Brutus, is not in our stars,
> But in ourselves, that we are underlings.'

No.	Page	
1	75	J. E. R. McDonagh: *The Nature of Disease*, 3 Vols. Heinemann.
2	75	A. D. Speransky: *The Basis for the Theory of Medicine*. Lawrence & Wishart.
3	76	The following material on morbid conditions of the vital body is reprinted with some modifications and omissions, from *Vital Magnetic Healing*, by A. Gardner, published by the Theosophical Research Centre.
4	81	Cf. McDonagh's description of fever. Op. cit. Vol. II, p. 5.
5	81	See under Physiotherapy.
6	86	Henderson and Gillespie: *Textbook of Psychiatry*. Oxford University Press.
7	88	For a description of obsessional conditions see *Man's Latent Powers*, pp. 203-209, by P. Payne. Faber & Faber.
8	89	M. Beddow Bayly: 'The Germ Theory of Disease', *Medical World*, June 15th, 1928; 'The Problem of Infection', *Medical World*, November 15th, 1929; *The Schick Inoculation*, National Anti-vaccination League, London; and *Natural Immunity*, The Health Education & Research Council, 15 St. James's Place, London.
9	90	Section compiled by M. Beddow Bayly.
10	91	*The Times*, January 22nd, 1926.

The following is an extract from this report, p. 15.

'For a quarter of a century it has been known that some, perhaps many, of the microbes which are individually responsible in a causal sense for definite and grave diseases in man and other animals are in themselves completely non-virulent. Introduced into the body in the absence of other agents they are quite harmless.

In disease due to organisms of several, perhaps of very many kinds, the disease begins only if special circumstances are present, in which some change in the body, due to some other factor than the infecting parasite itself, has been brought about. In such a case we are not dealing with a direct contest, so to speak, between host and parasite; the defence, or immunity, of the host is complete as against the parasite, so long as that is acting alone.'

| 11 | 92 | Pearson and Wyllie: *Recent Advances in Disease of Children*. Churchill. |
| 11A | 92 | *Medical Echo*, 1928, Vol. VI, No. 23, p. 49. |

No.	Page	
12	92	*A System of Bacteriology in Relation to Medicine,* Vol. III. H.M. Stationery Office, 1929. W. E. Gye and W. J. Purdy: *The Cause of Cancer,* p. 505. Cassell, 1931.
13	92	*Report to Medical Research Committee on Ventilation,* 1920.
14	92	*British Medical Journal,* November 3rd, 1928, p. 817.
15	92	The *Lancet,* August 4th, 1928, p. 214.
16	92	Ministry of Health *Report on Diphtheria,* No. 10, p. 13. C. B. Ker: *A Manual of Fevers,* p. 224. Oxford University Press.
17	92	Gill: *The Genesis of Epidemics,* p. 6. Baillière, Tindall & Cox, 1928. A. Brunel: *Les Idées Créatrices dans L'Evolution de la Médicine,* pp. 122-123. Bosc Frères, Lyons.
18	93	S. Guerney-Dixon: *The Transmutation of Bacteria.* Cambridge University Press. This is a standard work on the non-specificity of micro-organisms. The following quotation from page 90 fully bears out Dr. Kendall's contention that bacteria do not produce toxins in a medium containing excess of carbohydrate. 'The second observation is that in the case of some organisms—for example B. diphtheriae (Theobald Smith 1899, Fisher 1909)—toxins are formed in a culture only if the amount of sugar in the medium is very small—not more than a trace. . . . We find that some organisms, at any rate, do not elaborate toxins in the presence of much carbohydrate material.' J. W. H. Eyre: *Medical World,* February 14th, 1936, p. 797, on 'Adolescence and Microbial Infections', states: 'Bacteria tend to become a-virulent when they are implanted in an unsuitable "soil".'
19	93	J. E. R. McDonagh: *The Common Cold and Influenza.* Heinemann; especially introduction to Clinical and Bacteriological Sections, i.e., p. 5 and following, and 69 and following. W. R. Fearon: *Nutritional Factors in Disease,* p. 92. Heinemann.
20	94	The *Lancet,* March 10th, 1934, p. 523.
21	97	S. M. Mitra: *Anglo Indian Studies,* p. 326. Longmans, for Hindu views on effect of seasons on the medicinal properties of plants.

No. *Page*

L. Kolisko: *The Moon and the Growth of Plants*. Anthroposophical Publishing Co., London, 1938. We would somewhat query the validity of the conclusions drawn in this work as only one out of many possible, though hitherto unrecognized, factors has been considered.

22   97   See letter from W. A. Littel, the *Observer*, London, October 16th, 1927, concerning the effect of lunar phases upon timber.

23   98   A. Besant: *A Study in Karma*. Theosophical Publishing House, Madras, India.

C. Jinarajadasa: *Theosophy and Modern Thought*, Chap. I. Theosophical Publishing House, Madras, India.

24   100   H. Oertel: *Outline of Pathology*, p. 29. Renouf, Montreal, 1927.

25   101   See pages 29 *et seq*.

26   101   See under Diagnosis, pages 110 *et seq*.

27   101   See Introduction.

28   102   See under Correspondences, page 121.

29   103   See Suggestion, page 174.

30   104   See Osteopathy, page 138.

31   105   M. Beddow Bayly: 'The Basic Principles of Health and Disease', *Medical World*, July 6th, 1934.

Chapter V

DIAGNOSIS

W E come now to the question of diagnosis. This is
assessed against the background of the principles
set out in the preceding chapters.[1] It does not, of course,
exclude or deprecate the methods generally used, but
with some exceptions, endorses them.[2] On the other hand,
it takes these methods as offering only a partial view of
the patient, while a complete diagnosis must take into
account the *whole* person.

In chronic cases the first interview is of great importance in establishing a good rapport with the patient,
although in simple and in acute conditions—e.g. pneumonia or appendicitis—straightforward and immediate
attack upon the disease is all that is required. But when
one is called upon to treat complicated and chronic ill
health, it becomes necessary to go much more deeply and
more intimately into the whole situation. It is then most
helpful to encourage the patient to talk freely about his
troubles, as this quietly establishes a sympathetic rapport
between him and his doctor, and often is all that is needed
to start in the patient the process of self-healing.

When a good relationship has been established one can
be much more frank with the patient than one would
otherwise dare to be. This will tend to evoke a similar
honesty in the patient. A bridge is thus built which is
widely acknowledged to be the foundation of lasting
therapeutic work in all domains of medicine.

In the course of making a diagnosis a practitioner
should try to obtain certain information which can be
classified under four headings.

The four objectives to be held in mind as constituting
a satisfactory diagnosis are as follows:

I. To obtain a true clinical picture of the patient himself as a whole, including his physical and subtler bodies, his background, his environment, and his relationships to these.

II. To locate the primary seat of disease and of allied or secondary conditions either already developed or likely to appear, i.e. to make a thorough medical examination.

III. To obtain a clue to the kind of treatment likely to help both the symptoms and the root-causes of the disease.

IV. Wherever possible, to discover some means of helping the patient to re-orientate himself mentally and emotionally in order to keep well in the future. This state can rarely be reached at the first interview but may come as a result of many consultations and much discussion and in the light of an understanding of the deeper causes of disease. When such insight is lacking, or where the patient is likely to resist the suggestion of there being such deep subjective causes, it may be wise and even necessary to give up any attempt to deal radically with the trouble and to be content to treat the case merely as symptoms arise.

Each of the above points will now be considered in some detail. Many of them are obvious and platitudinous to any good physician, but they are included in order to complete the scheme. And as every doctor knows, there are many cases in which much of this elaboration is both useless and irrelevant.

I. To obtain a COMPLETE CLINICAL PICTURE of the patient one should note the following points:

(a) GENERAL APPEARANCE: age, build, colouring, stance, dress, set of eyes, mouth, shape of head, hands, feet.
Voice: quality, production, vocabulary.
Condition of body: nutrition, co-ordination, nervous movements, breathing (deep, shallow or rapid, etc.),

muscular tension (i.e. rigidity or relaxation of the body when at rest).

Social type: cultural development, intelligence, occupation.

(b) TEMPERAMENTAL CHARACTERISTICS: vital type (dense, fluid, nervous, bland); whether hypersensitive or insensitive.

Strength and stamina, muscular or nervous: i.e. is vitality chiefly centred at the physical level, giving abundant muscular energy, or does the patient draw on subtler (nervous) energies to keep going?

State of mind (surface condition): optimistic or pessimistic, normally or exaggeratedly; anxiety, depression, despair, etc.; co-operative or resistant to the physician.

Habits and appetites: types of food, sleep, cleanliness; exercise; sexual life; tobacco; alcohol, etc.

(c) FAMILY HISTORY: race and nationality; parents, heredity, ancestors, siblings; birthplace and places of residence and education.

(d) PERSONAL HISTORY: medical and psychological; financial conditions; dependents and responsibilities; shocks, accidents, operations, both recent and in early life.

II. MEDICAL EXAMINATION

(a) All the usual clinical and (where required and subject to the proviso made in subsequent chapters) laboratory methods should be used, and a clinical diagnosis made where possible. Special attention is needed in regard to the following:

Spinal abnormalities: localized tensions of muscles, soreness, tenderness or rigidity at any point. A good osteopathic chart may be of assistance.[3]

Metabolism: symptoms of endocrine unbalance, indicating possible disturbance of a chakram. Vagotonus or sympathicotonus: correlate with vital type, if possible. Stasis: local or general. Failure or excess of secretions. Intestinal fermentation and flatulence. *Condition of the most vital parts:* heart, lungs, etc., genitalia; autonomic nervous system.

Localized symptoms: character: sharp, dull, burning, throbbing, etc. Presence of vague moving pains (usually due to disturbances in vital body).

Amelioration and aggravation (see homoeopathic textbooks);[4] note time of day, motion, rest, heat, cold, lying down, dampness, dryness, etc.

(b) In attempting to locate the primary seat of disease and to determine its relation to secondary or allied conditions, which have developed or are likely to do so, the following questions arise:

Is the condition mainly physical? If so, is it due to under-nourishment; over-nourishment and wrong assimilation; wrong nourishment, i.e. deficiency of calcium, phosphates, vitamins, etc.; overwork, and exhaustion of function; structural lesions; wrong habits; lack of exercise, fresh air; over-clothing, etc.

Is the condition entirely physiological or reinforced by psychological causes, shock, anxiety, depression, etc.?

The relation of primary causes to secondary symptoms is one of the utmost importance, since many maladies continue to be considered intractable or even incurable because the treatments normally given are aimed at secondary rather than primary causes. In clinical practice the successful physician is often one who uses normal medical treatment to alleviate symptoms that have temporarily appeared at the surface in acute form, but who also succeeds, consciously or unconsciously, in relieving the patient's mind of anxiety on this or that point, and so gets down to the primary psychological factor that is acting as irritant and producing a stream of secondary symptoms for which a particular disease name is appropriate. The increase of nervous and 'rare' diseases, for which specific treatments are as rapidly manufactured by research chemists and forgotten by doctors after a few months, indicates the failure of modern methods to go back to the primary factors in disease causation and to deal with these.

III. To obtain a clue to the TYPE OF TREATMENT LIKELY TO HELP (a) THE SYMPTOMS; (b) THE ROOT-CAUSE OF THE DISEASE.

The practitioner should look for the source of emotional and mental disturbance in the background of all but acute disease. The latter must, of course, be treated primarily at the physical level, at any rate in the first instance.

As we have said, it is useful, even at the first interview, to attempt to determine something of the general vital condition of the patient, and to note whether the play of vitality is strong, with good resistance to disease, or whether it is slow, sluggish, and weak. If the patient's supply of vitality appears to be good and he seems likely to respond to physical treatments, and if he is also reasonably intelligent for his social environment, and co-operative, the practitioner need not concern himself much about deeper diagnosis of the subtler bodies.

If, on the other hand, vitality is low and resistance poor, or if the flow of vital energy (prāna) is noticeably erratic, or if the disease is chronic, the root of the trouble is almost certainly at the psychological level. Similarly, more deeply seated complications are likely to exist in the case which fails to respond to apparently suitable treatment, although the patient appears on the surface to be co-operative and truly anxious to get well. In all chronic and so-called incurable cases the psychological aspects should be taken into consideration: and if the case is suitable and circumstances permit, the patient may be referred to a reliable psychotherapist.[5] This, however, does not necessarily hold good where there is gross tissue change, even though the first real cause of the disease is plainly psychological.

In attempting to assess the vital condition of the patient the following points should be considered. The flow of vitality may be diminished for three reasons: (1) There may be a genuine exhaustion of vitality from direct over-work; (2) there may be a local block at some point; (3) there may be a psychological block causing a general sluggishness at the etheric level.

(1) If the condition of vital exhaustion is directly from over-use, what is the cause of this? Is it due to *circumstances*, i.e. actual need to overwork? Does it arise from an *emotional condition*: anxiety, fear, guilt, worry, etc., which drive the patient to overwork as an escape? Or from a *mental condition*: obsessive ideals; compulsions, repetitive actions, etc.; or to lack of mental efficiency and system?

(2) Where there is a local block in the flow of vitality, this may be a matter of a *localized physical condition*, such as those termed 'osteopathic lesions' (see *Osteopathy*, page 138), or it may be due to a psychological attitude affecting one area of the body only.

(3) Sometimes there is a *general condition of inertia*. In this condition ample energy is present but for some reason it is inactive and morbid rather than active and healthy. If the general flow of vitality is thus blocked, what is the inhibiting factor? Is it due to *frustration at the physical level*; lack of exercise or interest; a hedged-in life; maladjustment to sex and love-life, etc.? To *emotional* disappointment, shock, fixation, etc.? To *mental* rigidity, dissociation, absorption in phantasy, and so forth?

When the difficulty seems to be chiefly *emotional*, the physician should attempt to determine whether the person is normally of a negative, inert nature; lazy and self-indulgent; or normally 'outward-moving', but temporarily cramped or over-tired. The type of suggestion that may be successful, as well as the whole method of treatment, will differ for these divergent types.

If the check in the flow of vital energy seems to be mainly at the *mental* level, the problem may be one of structure and development. Is the patient mentally normal and of average intelligence? How clearly can he really think (i.e. orientation in time, place, etc.)? Is there a psychic maladjustment such as comes from prolonged dissociation, shock, or withdrawal such as occurs in dementia praecox? Is the mind strong though distorted; merely weak; weak and confused (as in alcoholic cases); inhibited or sluggish; active but restrained; over-stimulated?

A list of correspondences is given at the end of this chapter which may assist in arriving at a diagnosis on the lines indicated above.

IV. RE-ORIENTATION.

The attempt to assist the patient to re-orientate himself involves not only already familiar methods but also a knowledge of certain little known treatments which will be dealt with in Chapter VI.

SPECIAL TECHNIQUES

The present chapter would be incomplete if it did not include some mention of certain unusual diagnostic techniques which nowadays are coming into use in every country in the world. In many cases they are an unexplained capacity of a particular individual, but instances occur where a specially gifted person has been able to externalize his method and to make of it a communicable technique. In some cases machines for DIAGNOSIS BY RADIATIONS have been invented which at least a few practitioners, and often many, can use effectively. These machines vary from a simple divining rod, or pendulum, held in the practitioner's hands, to the most expensive electro-magnetic apparatus, with rheostats, amplifiers and specialized indicators. By means of such machines, and with or without a living subject, the radiations from the sputum, blood or saliva of a patient are said to be subjected to analysis. The inventors of the various types of apparatus have this in common, that they recognize the existence of subtle emanations from the human body. They also agree that these emanations vary, both in individuals and from time to time, the variations being indicative of health, sex and other conditions within the body.

One thing is certain, although it is by no means always admitted by practitioners using such machines. Whatever apparatus is used, simple or elaborate, it would not function without the conscious participation of the human operator. No diagnostic apparatus has yet (1948) been devised which eliminates the human factor. Moreover, it has been established that these apparatus continue to function even though electrically disconnected or under otherwise faulty conditions, according to the theory of their inventors, provided that the diagnostician does not realise the fault. In other words, provided his mental orientation is unaffected.

It follows from this that, no matter how helpful the apparatus may be as an objective focus, its efficacy depends upon the psychic ('psi') function of the operator, and not on any virtue in the pendulum or other apparatus itself. It is, in short, a means of focusing the psychic perceptivity of the user so that it works automatically.

Experimental work has also been conducted on orthodox lines in several research laboratories, proving that disease conditions within the body can be diagnosed through measuring the change in the electric potential at the surface of the body. In the work done at the Yale University School of Medicine the findings are said to make clear 'that the onset of adenocarcinoma of the mammary gland does something in the electrical pattern of the organism which can be measured with some degree of certainty'.[6]

The connection of the 'electrical pattern of the organism' with the functional entity to which we have given the name vital body is not yet demonstrated, but the behaviour of the two suggests a close association, and the use of delicate apparatus for the investigation of vital conditions is likely to impinge upon etheric phenomena.

So far as we can judge with our present knowledge, there is a genuine basis of fact which is common to all these machines and methods. The radiations of the vital aura certainly have specific qualities that indicate both healthy and unhealthy conditions. An over-active, lethargic or poisoned condition of the physical body has a characteristic radiation at the vital or electro-magnetic level which, if it can be isolated, correctly measured and read, will give an exact indication of the condition of the organ or part concerned. The clairvoyant with etheric sight sees the constant variations in these radiations, and learns to diagnose the conditions of the physical body by their colour, texture and rate. If changes in these emanations, which though subtle are still purely physical in nature, are as evident as this, they should be capable of mechanical measurement and record, provided that a machine is assembled sensitive enough to contact and differentiate their specific rates of activity.

In this connection it should be remembered that a diagnosis of vital conditions will not always coincide with the state at that moment established in the dense physical body, for although the vital form is closely allied to the dense physical, conditions can exist in the vital body before they appear physically,[7] and sometimes remain at the vital level after the physical condition appears cured. Ignorance regarding the level at which a machine is operating may easily lead to misjudgment of its accuracy, or to statements concerning results that over-reach the mark. The Boyd-Abrams Emanometer, however, was tested by a commission headed by Lord Horder in 1924, and was found to be one hundred per cent accurate on inorganic substances and with a high percentage of correct results on organic substances.[8]

One of the complications involved in the investigation of this and similar machines is that many of the operators undoubtedly possess some form of extra-sensory perception but, since this faculty is not yet scientifically acceptable, they are unwilling to admit that the machine is not the only factor concerned in the success of the method. They prefer to stress the scientific side of their work, ignoring the part played by the human body and personality, and hence are often unable to explain deviations in results which would have a normal explanation were these factors also considered. The success or failure of such diagnoses certainly does not depend wholly upon the machine used, but to some extent upon the vital type, the psychic sensitivity and the state of mind of the operator. To be successful such an operator needs, amongst other things, to make full use of the intuitional approach, rather than to depend wholly upon a too-critical intellect. Results can be critically examined at leisure, but in order to obtain consistently good results an operator has to learn to delete preconceptions and, during the process of diagnosis, to hold the mind open and still, as if divining the condition of the patient rather than using critical intelligence.

Such methods of diagnosis are still in their infancy. As they obviously depend upon some device which detects the behaviour of the vital body, a frank recognition of the existence of this body and its functionings in both operator and patient would do much to clarify the problems involved.

INTUITIVE FACULTY.[9] The existence of an intuitive capacity for diagnosis has always been recognized by the medical profession. The general practitioner is aware that among his colleagues are some who possess this faculty to a greater extent than others. He probably could not define it, nor does he as a rule regard it as something that can be trained and developed. Indeed, it may be questioned whether those who make use of their intuition for diagnostic work are themselves aware of the mechanism which they employ. Yet intuition has a specific mechanism that can be both understood and cultivated. For intuitive diagnosis it is not enough for the doctor to have a sympathetic understanding of human nature and its ills; in addition to this he needs a capacity for quick observation of detail and analogy, a good memory and the ability to enter into the consciousness of his patient. The same faculty is used by the scientist, philosopher or artist when, having given the best of his ordinary thinking to a problem, tension is released, and a leap made to a new and usually deeper and wider view of the whole matter. This ability to jump to a 'new' field is perhaps in itself what we mean by intuition.[10]

It may be a new idea to many that the intuitive faculty is one that can be consciously developed. Yet Professor C. G. Jung has said, like any other aspect of the mind, it can be developed by practice. Anyone who is born with this power can certainly increase it through constant use, and when the existence of the faculty is recognized and experiments made upon it, we may come to view it as a gift which, like any other, can be cultivated by suitable means.

A PSYCHIC FACULTY, or, as it is now called in scientific parlance, 'the psi function', is known to exist, and can be used in diagnosis, but it varies enormously in different people, ranging from an uncertain flair, which sometimes works and sometimes does not, through every degree of etheric psychometry and emotional or mental telepathy to the fully conscious use of trained clairvoyant capacity. The last named type of gift, when especially trained for medical work, is of great value both in clinical and research work. Unfortunately it is very rare; but as more becomes known about psychic powers, a larger number of workers could probably be developed and trained along these lines.[11]

There is a real danger in the use of uneducated psychic faculty for diagnosis, because the uninformed lay person is likely to be too easily impressed by the extra-sensory powers of the seer, and may be induced to follow a course of treatment, thereafter prescribed, which is based on psychic 'communications' or other non-qualified opinions —sometimes with fatal results. Extra-sensory methods of diagnosis are best used in connection with qualified medical practitioners, who can by their questions ensure that the clairvoyant has really seen the conditions described, can interpret their import, and because of training and experience can also direct the treatment upon sound lines.

At its best, clairvoyant diagnosis makes an important contribution to the study of disease conditions. A few clairvoyants exist who can actually see the organs at work inside the physical body, not merely as mechanical two-dimensional projections, as on the X-ray screen, but functioning in their normal places, with their vital emanations around them. Some clairvoyants are also able to make useful observations of the psychological and psychic states of the different bodies, vital, emotional and mental. They see, too, the condition of the chakras, and the play of thought and feeling through them. But even a naturally gifted clairvoyant of good type would be unable to make an accurate or complete diagnosis without considerable training, for although he might be able to see the diseased organs and twisted chakras he would usually not be capable of giving a correct interpretation of that which he had observed. In addition to his own special capacity he needs a knowledge of physiology, some experience of what the various organs and chakras look like when they are healthy, and accumulated experiences to enable him to interpret the deviations from normal.

It is obvious that even the best trained psychic should always work in conjunction with fully-trained medical practitioners, yet such co-operation between the psychic and the medically qualified person is by no means easy to establish. For one thing, the psychic needs open-mindedness and goodwill on the part of those with whom he is collaborating if he is to do his best work. Certain doctors will permit a patient to have a psychic diagnosis out of curiosity, meanwhile maintaining a critical and even hostile attitude towards the psychic observer. This hinders good work, as the clairvoyant has to cope with the doctor's resistance as well as deal with the case. Other practitioners may be more open in attitude, but if the psychic's description does not tally with their own opinion they will persist in treatment which altogether ignores the advice given.

Their lack of knowledge in regard to the very existence of vital and psychological structures invalidates for them even the possibility of the diagnosis being correct if the opinion expressed differs from their own. Once the possibility of psychic diagnosis is admitted by the medical world many of these difficulties will disappear.

CORRESPONDENCES

Since reliable psychics are rare, and the value of untrained psychic faculty is open to question, the use of a system of correspondences between the psychological states and physical disorders is often illuminating.

The following is a list of correspondences between physical functions, organs, areas, and allied emotional and mental states. We cannot here reproduce the case records upon which many of the statements are based. Such records exist and are accumulating. The correspondences have been drawn from many sources, however, and are not wholly empirical. We have recorded them as an assistance in diagnosis, since a fixed psychological attitude noted in a patient may frequently be used as a true key to deeply-hidden physical disorder; while fixed physiological conditions, resistant to ordinary medical treatment, may yield to an attack upon their corresponding—and frequently causative—psychological state.

In making a diagnosis on the basis of correspondences the practitioner must in each case use his own intuition and best judgment: there cannot be a fixed rule governing such subtle matters. Correct diagnosis through the use of correspondences demands the right estimation of a syndrome, in which various lines of influence of unequal significance impinge upon a particular physical area. The correspondences as here given have been found to hold true in a large number of cases: they have been well tested in clinical experience, yet a shallow or hasty application of any one of them in a given instance might lead to an utterly false conclusion. On the other hand, an open minded search for the true psychic correspondence in a specially intricate case will frequently result in the discovery of a well known and previously noted relationship.

We have divided the list into two main groups, which we have called TISSUE OR EMBRYOLOGICAL and REGIONAL OR ANATOMICAL. According to the type of the patient and the material of which his different bodies are made one group or the other will tend to dominate a syndrome: moreover, a given symptom cannot always be attributed to the same psychological cause. For instance, in nervous indigestion both the region of the stomach and the nervous system are involved. Nerve pains are connected ultimately with some form of mental tension, the central nervous system, in general, corresponding with the mind. This is a tissue correspondence. But the region of the stomach is directly under the influence of the emotions, for the solar plexus ganglion and chakram react directly to emotional stimuli. This is a regional correspondence. A close relationship between mind and emotion is obviously involved in all such conditions, and it becomes a question as to which of the two is bringing the greater pressure to bear upon the physical organism.

Another important principle involved is that the whole of nature is built up in terms of pairs of opposites, the members of each pair having a very close relation to each other.[12] Hence opposite extremes of the same attitude may produce similar symptoms, either through over-activity of a certain function or by exhaustion and under-activity of its opposite, the inhibiting and balancing function. For example, both extreme egoism and extreme shyness affect the spine; while excessive activity—or desire for activity—and laziness both ultimately check the flow of prāna, both producing approximately the same result. In many cases, consequently, apparent opposites will be found under the same heading and, in the list that follows, when they are not specifically mentioned they may be taken for granted.

The two groups of tissue and regional correspondences evidently cut across one another, and illness is apt to occur at points of intersection, where correspondences in the two groups impinge upon one area or organ. For example, a psychic etiological factor corresponding to bony tissue in the first group, such as an attitude of extreme obstinacy or fixity, and another from the second group corresponding to the hip-joint, such as non-acceptance of physical experience, can lead to osteo-arthritis in the hip. Similarly, an over-strained vagus nerve induced by misuse of the will may affect the throat, heart, adrenals or pancreas, according as these organs are strengthened or weakened by psychological factors which affect their anatomy.

1. Embryological or Tissue Correspondences

These divide up into the three familiar groups based on the embryology of the tissues concerned, as follows:

(a) *Mesodermic Group: bones, muscles, ligaments, fascia, etc.* These correspond and react to will and to the sense of self, or I-ness, and are connected with physical activity. The spine, particularly, may be affected by all forms of egoism, including pride, shyness and all inferiority feelings.

(b) *Endodermic Group: mucosa of viscera, and fluids connected with them; chyle, mucus, bile, gastric juice, urine, etc.* In general, this group corresponds and reacts to the emotional life, though mental strain working through the nerves in a particular part of the body will affect the secretion of fluids in that region.

(c) *Ectodermic Group: Brain, Spinal Cord, nerves, skin, etc.* These are connected with mental stimuli, the cerbro-spinal system being directly influenced by thought itself, the sympathetic by thought plus emotion, and the para-sympathetic by thought plus the will and forms of creative activity. The vagal section and cortex of the brain are also directly influenced by meditation, etc., which also profoundly affects the hypothalamus. This means that properly directed mental activity, as well as meditation, can help disturbed nervous function in the head, whereas over-intensity in mental activity may lead to cerebral or vagal irritation and exhaustion and sometimes affect the sacral para-sympathetic group as well.

II. REGIONAL CORRESPONDENCES

Head. The head, in general, represents man's power to direct himself, hence psychological disturbance connected with one's capacity to face life effectively and intelligently registers as head strain and local nervous disorder. Headaches across the forehead and certain types of eyestrain indicate anxiety or unwillingness to face facts that need to be faced or seen. The top of the head is allied to overstrain in regard to sex, to power, and to spiritual aspiration or ambition. The occipital area registers overconfidence as well as the type of anxiety, as 'Can I get through with this?'

Eyes. In connection with the eyes there is a wide range or correspondences relating directly to the mind. The psychic state at any moment can be seen by a close observer to register in minute changes in the refractive powers of the eye, and sustained psychic states tend to be reflected in fixed conditions in the same organ. There are also a whole series relating to the complicated structure of the eye and its surrounding tissues, as well as to changes in expression and pupillary, refractive and retinal changes. We cannot here go into details in regard to this very complicated matter, which is a complete science in itself. There are practitioners who claim to make a diagnosis of a patient's physical condition by examination of the eye alone, and they are often remarkably accurate in their findings, though it would seem that in most of them a strong intuitive factor is at work.

As a small but important point in diagnosis it is useful to remember that the circulation in the eye is largely determined by spinal conditions at the first thoracic level, through the effect of these upon the autonomic system.

Hence a psychological tension concerning responsibilities (see *Shoulders* below) may develop a secondary condition of eye strain.

Nose. Discrimination, or the lack of it, is the psychological correspondence for the nose. It is also connected with sex and with the sense of power and domination. The brow chakram (in the forehead) is the centre that registers the activity of the higher ranges of directive capacity and perceptive powers, whether consciously psychic, intellectually conscious, or instinctive. The nerves and tissues of the nose and of the antra are affected by disorders and overstrains in this chakram.

Ears. Anxiety to hear and dislike of hearing, as well as certain forms of inquisitiveness and of retreat from life, register in nervous disorder in the region of the ears. Noises in the ears, when not due to high blood pressure or a foreign body, indicate local overstrain in the vital body or, frequently, fastidiousness and the sense of self-importance.

Mouth. For this there is a wide range of correspondences to do with digestion, assimilation, and give-and-take in life. Sometimes frustrated power and consequent impatience affect the tongue. As psychologists know, there is a direct connection also between the mouth and sexual life. Lips, teeth and tongue each have their own special correspondences. Disorders of the mouth should be considered in connection with the throat.

Tonsils and Adenoids. The correspondences for these bodies are a complicated subject, as they represent a junction between mesoderm and endoderm, and hence embryologically represent an interplay of will and emotion. From the regional, or anatomical, point of view, they lie between the mouth and the throat, and so are concerned with the assimilation of experience and conflicts with environment. Children developing adenoids may do so for a wide variety of psychological reasons, as well as from improper diet.

Throat, with Thyroid and Parathyroid Glands. The neck

is also very complex in its correspondences, since it serves as a meeting point for many forms of energy. It is a bridge between ingoing and outgoing forces and involves the relationship between the subjective and the objective worlds of a patient, as well as that between his conscious life and his environment. Typical difficulties both of the throat tissues and of the thyroid gland arise from fear of self-expression and inability to express oneself; sexual disturbances, both in regard to excess and to retreat from sexual life; rebellion against environment; a sense of frustration. Throat difficulties occur usually in the more intellectual patients, and it is useful to make a comparison between them and the gastro-intestinal disturbances of predominantly emotional people. The quality of the voice is always indicative of the state of the psyche, for it grows shrill with anxiety, is broken by suppressed emotion, and becomes artificial when the patient feels defensive or insecure or is exerting very rigid control. A free, open throat and full-toned voice indicate ease in handling emotional experience.

Shoulders. Difficulties within this area indicate that the attitude towards responsibility should be examined. For example, the man who shoulders his way through life may develop rheumatism in a shoulder joint, while the school teacher who feels her burden too heavy easily gets cramp in the back of the neck. The first thoracic vertebra is affected by both these attitudes, and heart troubles, lung troubles (through the first pulmonary plexus), and indigestion, can all be secondary reactions to a shoulder strain. (See also above under *Eyes*.)

Hands and Arms. These are related to the power to grasp and use opportunities, or fear of the lack of opportunities, as well as aggressiveness in action, tenacity in regard to things, and exactingness. The latter attitudes sometimes result in writer's-cramp.

Heart. Over-confidence and its opposite, anxiety, affect the heart directly. 'An anxiety heart' is a phrase occasionally used colloquially in medical circles. Frustration in self-expression would probably register first at the throat chakram and affect the upper thoracic area, and from thence affect the heart, whereas direct frustration of emotional life may register in the heart chakram, especially when the love nature, as distinct from the sex nature, is frustrated. In more evolved types, the heart also corresponds on its nervous and muscular side, i.e. as a pump, to the concrete mind. Mental rigidity as well as its opposite, too great flexibility, or a lack of mental stamina, can be the psychological basis of valvular heart trouble. Conflicts regarding the power to sense truth and to express it also register in the heart chakram.

Lungs. In general, breathing reflects the whole attitude to life. Short, quick breaths indicate fear and over-eagerness; medium deep breathing indicates normal self-confidence and assurance; deep, full breathing shows a high degree of poise and, if unassumed, of inner serenity. Variations in breathing, such as sudden gasps and checks, should be closely noted for diagnostic purposes. For example, a stationary diaphragm is often due to rigidity in the solar plexus chakram, i.e. to emotional stasis of some sort. Lung troubles correspond frequently to avidity for experience or, conversely, to lack of motive in life. The idea that the tuberculous patient is bright and cheerful needs examination: such an attitude is often compensatory for deep-seated insecurity and inability to face the adaptation required for existence in the given circumstances.

Digestive Organs. The correspondences for these are so elaborate that they will be given in some detail. In general the whole digestive system, from mouth including teeth, salivary glands, etc., to excretory organs, indicates various aspects of the capacity to select, assimilate and delete information and personal experience.

> *The stomach*—The digestive juices, nerves and muscles of the stomach are affected by emotional states through the solar plexus chakram.

> *The pancreas and adrenals*—The pancreas seems to have a special psychological connection with the

para-sympathetic system through the vagus nerve, for its disturbed conditions are closely connected with the use of the will and the power to relax tension or to sustain it voluntarily. The adrenals react more directly to the sympathetic nervous system and thus to emotion. These two groups should be in a state of balance. Malfunction of one group usually involves the other, and both react on the liver.

The liver—This is affected by criticism, resentment, aggression and irritability, either conscious or unconscious, and their opposites. The 'peace at any price' person frequently develops liver trouble.

The pylorus—This area reacts immediately to fear, through the sympathetic nervous system. Pyloric cramp is an important reaction to a cramp in the solar plexus chakram. Acute cramp, induced psychologically, can easily be mistaken for ulceration, and vice versa.

The intestines—Psychological states, such as a lack of discrimination, avidity, miserliness, fear of not having enough, clinging to unnecessary and outgrown things and ideas, all affect the function of the large and small intestines. Excellent examples are the constipated miser and the dissatisfied colitis case. The villi of the intestinal lining are largely mesodermic (i.e. will and power sense), but they pass their secretions through to endodermic tissue (affected by emotion).

The spleen—The spleen reflects the general attitude to life, as such: it is affected by one's personal sense of importance or inadequacy; by one's capacity or incapacity to draw on the universal supply of life-energy.

NOTE: All correspondences given for the abdominal organs should be considered in the light of the general condition of the solar plexus, both nervous and vital, and of the blood stream.

The solar plexus—The solar plexus registers the whole of the emotional life and pours emotional influences into the middle belt of the physical body through the medium of the solar plexus ganglion and its connections. Hence the middle area of the body reacts readily to all emotional disturbance, the nerves and muscles in the area becoming rigid through shock or collapsed through depression, strain, etc.

The kidneys—As the kidneys are selective in function and yet deal with fluid excretion, it is the more emotional attitude towards discrimination which registers here—states such as emotional confusion, lack of insight, lack of selectivity. For comparison note that purely intellectual criticism, possibly with emotion regarding it unconsciously suppressed, affects the nose, while tendencies to uncritical reiteration or over critical resentment register in the liver and intestines.

The anus—Conditions here reflect the will and the creative life, also fear of distorted interest with regard to sex, i.e. those levels known to Freudian psychologists as anal-erotic. This is due in part to the close proximity of the root chakram at the base of the spine. Fixed refusal to get rid of deep prejudices, resentment, etc., may also affect the functional capacity of the anus.

Genital Organs. These organs have their obvious correspondences in creative activity, but they react especially to the patient's attitude towards sex, to resentment due to sexual frustration, shock, distaste, etc. Certain menstrual difficulties are often caused by an osteopathic lesion, particularly at the level of the fifth lumbar vertebra; yet osteopathy may fail unless a psychological readjustment is also made towards a greater freedom or sincerity of attitude concerning sex. Recurrent irritability of the anus or vagina, and other local sensations, may reflect a distorted attitude towards evacuation and the sex functions, as well as to an alteration of endocrine balance from any cause.

Thighs. The area of the thighs reacts to genital correspondences but in a less specialized manner. Bony disease in the thighs, especially if it impedes walking, is more likely to correspond to will than to sex, particularly if the chakram at the base of the spine is involved. One of the dangers of X-ray treatment for menstrual difficulties is that of an induced disorder of this chakram, with consequent loss of power, or other symptoms, in the area of the thighs. Sciatica may result from sexual frustration or abnormality, or from mental anxiety in regard to creative capacity, whether sexual or otherwise. Or it may be simply mechanical in origin, as in lesions of displacement or pressure in the pelvic area.

The various forms of spastic paralysis are frequently associated with a frustrated will, lack of will power, or excessive use of it.

Knees. The knees are affected by fear or over-confidence, particularly when undertaking new work, and also by a general sense of insecurity.

Feet. These may react to insecurity or to over-confidence at a more basic level. 'Feeling the ground firm beneath one's feet' is an indicative phrase. Lack of mental co-ordination and obstinacy sometimes affect the feet. We speak of 'digging one's feet in'.

Growths in any part of the body—In general, growths indicate that either mind or emotions have become fixated psychologically in the area corresponding to that in which the growth appears. Malignant growths may have as their basis some deep anxiety or resentment, more often unconscious than conscious and consequently very hard to discover and to treat. A piece of the unconscious has, as it were, walled itself off, and the dissociated vital structures return to an embryonic condition because isolated. This is, however, a highly complex subject and no full explanation is as yet known to us.

SPECIAL CORRESPONDENCES.

Lymphatic vessels. The lymphatics correspond in part to the mesodermic group (will, self, I-ness), but they are also closely associated with the fluids of the body and hence register emotional states, particularly those associated with stubbornness, emotional drive, or other forms of rigid or suppressed desire.

Endocrine glands. As would be expected from their embryonic origin, these glands show complicated reactions and should be considered in the light of the origin of the particular part involved. References can be made to the chart, page 40, showing chakras, glands and area affected.

No.	Page	
1	109	The point of view expressed in this section, as well as some of the detail, is derived in part from a study of the Ayurvedic, or traditional Hindu, system of medicine. See Reference No. 2, Chapter III.
2	109	J. W. Murray: *Examination of the Patient and Symptomatic Diagnosis*, 2nd edition. Kimpton, 1936.
		This remarkably thorough outline of what is required for a complete medical examination recognizes the value of many points which have been stressed in the present work. Amongst others note the comment on the attitude of the doctor to the patient at the first interview, pages 18-21, and the importance of including psychological factors, page 25.
3	111	See under Osteopathy, p. 151.
4	112	Homoeopathic manuals give these in detail. See, for example, Neatly and Stonham: *Manual of Homoeopathic Therapeutics*, pp. 961-1084. Bale and Danielsson.
5	113	J. W. Murray: Op. cit., p. 25.
6	116	*Science Digest*, Vol. III, No. 6, June, 1928, p. 28: 'Electrical Diagnosis of Brain Lesions', p. 68: 'Possible Electrical Method for Diagnosing Cancer'. Also recent literature on Encephalography.
7	117	Op. cit.
8	117	See Report in *British Medical Journal*, Jan. 24th, 1925, p. 179.
9	118	Cf. J. H. van der Hoop: 'Intuition in Medical Psychology', *British Journal of Medical Psychology*, Vol. XVI, Parts 3 and 4, p. 255.
10	119	Cf. C. Spearman's theory of insight. *Creative Mind*. Cambridge University Press; also Francis Aveling: *Psychology: The Changing Outlook*, pp. 26-31. Watts.
		Francis Aveling: *Personality and the Will*, pp. 180-182, 238-239. Cambridge University Press.
		K. W. Wyle: *Intuition*. Cambridge University Press.
		Alexis Carrel: *Man, the Unknown*, pp. 121-124. Hamish Hamilton.
11	119	P. Payne: *Man's Latent Powers*, Chaps. IX and X. Faber & Faber.
		L. J. Bendit: *Paranormal Cognition*. Faber & Faber.
12	122	In physics the balance between opposites is evident in the atom where the relationship between so-called positive and negative poles of electricity is the basis of stability. In plant life this principle is manifest in the polarity of cell division, while the growth cycle takes place through the interplay of katabolic and anabolic forces. In animal forms the behaviour pattern is conditioned by the polarity of sex, etc.

Chapter VI

PRINCIPLES OF TREATMENT

G ENERAL REMARKS. A student of medicine who is following the line of approach indicated in this book will base his selection of treatments in a given case upon certain clearly defined principles. He will fully accept the fact that there is a natural and well established tendency in both mind and body towards the preservation and restoration of health: *vis medicatrix naturae*. In treatment, therefore, his task is (1) to conserve that natural tendency, (2) to remove obstacles to its action, (3) on occasion to restore it by suitable stimuli, (4) to use as little as will well fulfil the purpose extrinsic or synthetic preparations to take the place of normal metabolic products, with a preference for natural products as against synthetic unless the former are less efficient. In more explicit terms, he will do all he can to draw upon the patient's normal source of vitality and to free the flow of that vitality from any hindrances which may inhibit its active functioning. At the same time he will avoid administering gland extracts or artificial foods unless clearly indicated, preferring to supply chemical deficiencies through carefully selected diet, as this enables the bodily forces more readily to restore the balance of metabolism. His approach being thus vitalistic rather than mechanistic, he avoids where possible any form of treatment or laboratory investigation that lowers the patient's resistance, or even temporarily dislocates the normal metabolic balance. Such investigations are often made, or artificially-stimulating treatments given, regardless of the power of the organism to cope with or to sustain the change induced by the artificial means employed. A lumbar puncture, for instance, from the point of view of the vital currents is far from being the harmless thing it is usually thought to be, though it may at times be necessary to relieve pressure on the brain, or for diagnosis which cannot otherwise be made.

While acknowledging that vaccination and preventive inoculations undoubtedly help to prevent epidemics of certain diseases, he will recognize also the many failures, as well as the risk of protein shock, etc., which may occur. He will therefore have to consider the relative advantages and disadvantages in any situation calling for them, and choose accordingly.

He will also try to avoid such practices as excessive X-ray investigation because of the destructive effect of these rays on cell life in general; the Schick test in connection with diphtheria; and all operations, unless clearly indicated, where a surgical incision is made in order to remove pieces of tissue from deep-lying parts of the body for the purpose of seeing whether they are healthy or not. Such practices all lower resistance and disturb important vital processes. There is a tendency to treat such investigation too lightly and to ignore the far-reaching effects of anaesthetics and surgical shock upon vital processes in general and the derangement caused to the ordinary functional activities by even slight instrumental interference.

The patient should not be envisaged as a laboratory experiment with certain physical data to work upon, but seen as a whole—body, soul, and spirit—hence the aim should be to help him to adjust his own mechanism to his own individual norm, and in doing this to enable him to make a healthy reaction to his environment.

Having this point of view, a doctor naturally selects methods of treatment (1) which help the normal elimination of toxins, such as diet, skin and bowel therapy, breathing and relaxation, etc., including suitable medicines when necessary, and (2) those which stimulate to normal activity organs which are sluggish, these reacting back into the first group and assisting in elimination.

Such treatments are manipulative treatments; electro-therapy; ray-therapy, including colour-treatments; vital magnetic treatments; and suitable tonic medicines, particularly those that fill a temporary deficiency, such as ampoules of calcium, phosphorus and iron, together with the 'trace' metals (copper and manganese), and preparations of iodine, vitamin concentrates, etc. (3) He will also consider the psychological causes that predispose his patient to disease and the factors in the environment which are involved in the same question, and he will use whatever methods are available to adjust the environment more favourably to the patient or to assist the latter to make a suitable adjustment within himself.

This is an exacting standard of treatment for each individual case, and applies perhaps more usefully to chronic than to acute conditions. In general, acute diseases, such as rheumatic fever or tonsilitis, yield to treatment of symptoms more readily than do chronic conditions. At the same time, even acute ailments in some individuals respond readily to certain forms of psychotherapy, while all of them yield to simple eliminative treatment, in addition to any specific remedy that may be indicated.

1. TREATMENT OF ACUTE DISEASES

Even in the treatment of acute disease the general principles outlined above should be adhered to as far as possible. Acute diseases, usually spoken of as acute infections, are probably all the result of an accumulation of waste and toxic matter in the system coming in contact with some factor that acts as a precipitant. This contact brings about the crisis we term an acute infection. It is roughly like the bursting of a dyke or the boiling over of a kettle. During the crisis the vital pores endeavour to eliminate the accumulated waste as rapidly as possible, and as this is done more efficiently under an increased temperature, fever supervenes.

FEVERS. In fevers of all kinds the first requisite is there-

fore to assist elimination, and it is well to give a brisk
purge at the onset to empty the alimentary canal. Some
therapists claim that there is nothing better for fever than
the cold pack, applied to the whole body once or twice a
day to promote perspiration without accompanying
exhaustion; and as some constitutions would find this too
drastic, tepid sponging may be substituted, with benefit
both to the skin and the central nervous system at the
same time as hot drinks of fruit juice and water are
administered (see under Hydrotherapy below).

Such diseases as tonsilitis, diphtheria, the common cold
and influenza occasionally respond spectacularly to such
treatment. Since a great deal of the waste matter in all
fevers is acid in character, such drugs as potassium citrate
and potassium tartrate, given in a half to one teaspoonful
doses in water or fruit drinks, help, by their alkaline
nature, to eliminate toxins and neutralize their irritating
properties; at the same time they preserve the alkaline
reserves of the body and promote diuresis as well as
sweating. It should perhaps be mentioned here that
homoeopathic preparations of drugs, salts, etc., do not
replace mineral loss from the body, owing to the amount
of the dose being infinitesimal. Rather, they act on the
disorganized radiations which occur in diseased states,
neutralizing them, and stimulating organs into healthy
activity by intensifying their normal rhythm (see under
Homoeopathy below). Such homoeopathic remedies as
aconite, belladonna, bryonia, gelsemium, rhus, etc., are
used effectively in common fevers.

For all feverish conditions, save those where exhaustion
demands special nourishment, fruit juices and the fibrous
flesh of fruits, Marmite and vegetable broth with vegetables other than the pulses incorporated in it[1] should be
substituted for milky foods or meat soups, as they enable
the body to throw off the toxic conditions while at the
same time supplying a certain amount of chemical energy.
When the acute stage is past, body-building foods, such
as cereals, nuts and dairy produce, may be added to the

eliminative diet as the patient gradually enters the convalescent stage. In practice the patient's inclination is often the best guide, provided always that he will take in as much fluid as can be reasonably tolerated.

We now come to a brief discussion of particular treatments. These in most instances can only be named and our point of view indicated. References will be given to enable the practitioner to obtain fuller information when desired. In the next chapter a few typical cases will be described which have actually been treated by these methods. No one form of treatment is likely to effect a permanent cure or change of habit in the body; it is the skilful use of a combination of treatments which attack the disease conditions on all levels, physical, vital, and psychological, which at times has produced very striking results.

ii. Surgery

When essential, surgical treatments should be used in the ordinary way, but every possible effort should be made to avoid surgical interference with the body because shock, the likelihood of adhesions forming and the difficulty in obtaining really good convalescent conditions for the vital body, make operations most undesirable. Any operation which involves an anaesthetic throws the whole vital body into confusion. A vigorous animal body may return to normal fairly easily, but the over-medicated, toxin-producing bodies of nervous and over-stimulated mankind to-day do not do so to anything like the extent that the mechanistic physician believes. Immediate relief and apparent recovery from shock may be noted, but not the failure of the bodily tissues to return in the long run to their rhythm. It is the family physician who has the best chance of estimating these matters.[2] Some of the methods indicated below are not yet well known, and yet they frequently have been successful in avoiding an operation even where it seemed to be inevitable.

III. PHYSIOTHERAPY

MANIPULATIVE TREATMENTS. The benefits of manipulative treatments are sometimes very dramatic. As our basic proposition is that life should be freed to do its own work in the body, we consider it to be of fundamental importance that any constriction or abnormal hindrance to the flow of that life should be removed as speedily as possible, and in such a way as to ensure that the surrounding tissues are re-educated to perform their respective tasks effectively.

The healthy flow of vital forces in any area depends upon a normal relationship of tissues in that area, as well as upon freedom from structural interference with the nerves themselves for the flow of prāna from the spine is not only channelled along the fatty sheaths of the nerve fibres but runs over the tissues and through them independently of the nerves. Congested tissue around an organ can and frequently does hold back the normal vital discharges, and the consequent congestion throws the organic activities into disorder.

MASSAGE is a treatment which can relieve congestions of this nature, and in treating the conditions in the dense physical body, for which its use is so widely recognized, a masseuse often gives direct relief to conditions of vital congestion or depletion. The value of massage is so well established in this and other countries that it needs no further comment. A good masseuse interested in vital magnetic healing (see below) or who, while using the orthodox technique, unconsciously treats vital conditions, is of great value to any general practitioner.

OSTEOPATHY. Conditions where the flow of vitality is inhibited may arise directly from structural distortion of the vertebral column, such as occurs in accidents or from bad posture habits; or may indirectly arise from local strains, congestions, etc., which inhibit circulation of blood, nervous energy and prāna in a special area. The osteopathic technique has been developed to release ten-

sion in and around the spine, so that the organs and areas
of the whole body may continue to receive the benefit of
a freely-functioning nervous system. The vertebrae from
which emerge the nerves associated with a given organ or
area are those specially treated when disease in that organ
or area is present. For further description, comment and
evidence readers are referred to osteopathic textbooks.[3]

It is not generally known outside America that osteopathic qualifications in many American States are as
exacting as those of the orthodox medical schools. In
others, unfortunately, the requirements for registration
are of very low standard compared to those in Great
Britain. There are, however, several highly equipped
colleges of osteopathy with large hospitals attached, and
in an increasing number of cities the municipal hospitals
have osteopathic wings where diseases of all kinds are
treated by manipulation, diet and, when necessary, other
methods, an osteopathic practitioner being in charge.
Excellent results are obtained. Owing to ignorance, and
to the lack in Great Britain of any recognized osteopathic
body to whom to turn for a standard of reference, practitioners abound in this country who would not be allowed
to practise where the profession is more properly regu-
lated. *Great care should therefore be taken in referring
patients for treatment* (quite apart from the legal and
medical question of etiquette and status), for while the
work of the fully qualified and hospital-trained osteopath
is likely to be as cautious, intelligent and sincere as that
of a medical man trained on orthodox lines, the work of
the semi-qualified practitioner, unless the individual has
some special personal gift, is likely to do as much harm
as good.

The value of manipulative surgery is becoming recognized in the hospitals of this country, and an increasing
number of treatments which are equivalent to the osteopathic, are being given by surgeons and physicians.[4]
Sometimes, however, it is apt to be rather rough and ready,
especially when done under anaesthesia, and only too often

it fails badly when compared with the delicate work of a good osteopath. Under whatever label this treatment is administered the basic principle is the same.

The treatment is not as well known as some others. But it may bring about spectacular results in intractable cases which have failed to yield to ordinary methods. Many of the typical cases listed below do yield rapidly to the usual treatment, or even cure themselves. But the right kind of manipulation may, if given in time, prevent an acute condition becoming chronic, or cut short the duration of the trouble.

Neuritis and Neuralgia. Osteopathy is useful in cases where there is congestion and tenderness at the point in the spine where the nerves affected make their connection —provided, of course, that there is no suggestion of tuberculous or other organic disease.

Functional Digestive, Respiratory, and Cardiac Cases. These have been known to yield spectacularly to osteopathy. Heart cases, however, require great caution where the upper thoracic region of the spine is affected. Sympathetic plexuses are involved which give secondary, if not primary, responses to the spinal adjustment.

Chronic asthma occasionally yields to osteopathy.

Dyspepsia due to atony or to spasm of stomach or bowel can be helped by manipulation of the dorsal vertebrae.

Malfunction in the Genital Areas, menstrual pain, etc., also *sciatica* and *coccydynia.* These are often associated with very slight pelvic twists.

Local Pain after an accident, not always in the area obviously affected, and the cause for which is not traceable by the ordinary orthopaedic specialist, can frequently be cured by osteopathic adjustment. For example, partial blindness following an accident, when the visual mechanism itself is uninjured, may sometimes be traced to a lesion in the upper cervical region, probably the first vertebra. Adjustment in that area has been known to produce remarkable results.

Post-Operative Conditions, Shock, etc. If there is a vague general discomfort and slow recovery following an operation, fall or other accident, or shock, and these do not yield to methods for restoring vital circulation (see below), it is useful to have an osteopathic opinion as to the possible cause. Deep massage does not by any means take the place of skilled osteopathic adjustment, though deep spinal massage is a useful substitute if no qualified osteopath is available.

Persistent Headache and Backache should be treated by this method if obtainable. A general practitioner can often relieve a headache by applying gentle traction to the head and neck.

REMEDIAL EXERCISES. The value of these exercises for structural defect and bad posture habits is fully recognized, but there are very few patients who do not need at least to be reminded about deeper and more rhythmic breathing, as well as to be given some instruction about relaxation. This is best done by well-trained and qualified teachers of remedial exercises. There are a number of good methods besides those of the generally accepted Swedish school. Those who have recognized the importance of the condition of the vital body will appreciate the value of good breathing habits. The supply of vitality in the body is directly dependent upon the use of full lung capacity, so that the establishment of deep and easy breathing is of the utmost importance for all invalids. Physical posture and nervous or psychological tensions often constrict the breath to a minimum intake, or, if the intake is fair, limit the circulation of vitality unduly. As the flow of prāna takes place largely over the nerve sheaths, any constriction, physical or psychological, which inhibits the flow along the nerves or over local tissues, decreases the supply of vitality in the area influenced by the nerves in question and inhibits the normal functions of cell life. Many nervous disorders cure themselves if the flow of nervous vitality can be restored in the given area.

In regard to relaxation, the work of Dr. Edmond Jacobson of Chicago University on the curative effects of deep relaxation is well known, though not enough use has yet been made of his technique.[5] Indigestion, insomnia, gastritis, colitis, as well as chronic nervous exhaustion will at times yield to this treatment, if this is combined with correct diet and with assistance given to the patient to aid him to take a more constructive view of life. The actual experience on the part of the patient of taking his own body in hand and making it relax and breathe as required, is evidently part of the curative process, although Dr. Jacobson does not stress this point. The greatest obstacle to achieving success along such lines will often be found to be the patient's resistance to taking any responsibility at all for his own recovery, and his feeling, conscious or unconscious, that 'nothing I can do for myself is ever any good'. If the doctor uses a little ingenuity, patience and right suggestion in convincing such an invalid that the regular practice of necessary exercises has value he may well be rewarded by achieving a cure where other and perhaps more spectacular methods have failed.

Failure to get significant results in suitable cases will probably be due to one or other of the following causes: deep psychological problems in the patient beyond the reach of physiotherapy; lack of persistence in practice; or a failure correctly to understand and apply the technique.

DIET. Since the body is an inherently healthy organism capable of self-maintenance if properly handled, the nature and quality of the food, water and air by which that body must sustain its activities at the physical level is of obvious importance.

One of the gaps in orthodox medical training, which is only now beginning to be filled, is the lack of emphasis upon the processes of metabolism and absence of detailed instruction in regard to the effects of special diets upon health.

Modern biochemical analysis has shown metabolic processes to be extremely intricate and to demand special scientific knowledge for their adequate comprehension. The perfect book on diet, presenting this subject in a clear and comprehensible form for the general practitioner, has yet to be written, although several which are contributive and valuable are given in our bibliography.

SYNTHETIC FOODS. Patent, bottled, and concentrated foods are apt to be good food denatured and devitalized, and hence lack something of great importance which fresh foods possess and which is not compensated for or restored by artificial irradiation. Very intense heat dissipates the etheric double, and this may be the factor involved, for, at the etheric level, dried concentrated food and fresh are of totally different appearance and the concentrated food has far less vitalizing power.

Nowadays it is recognized that certain elements contained in complex compounds supplied by the plant kingdom are more readily assimilable than the same elements obtained from a simple inorganic salt. This indicates that some obscure vital or structural quality is added by the incorporation of the mineral in the protoplasm of a living cell. Thus synthetic drugs are known to be inferior in their physical effect to the same compound as it occurs in nature, for although the synthetic product may be chemically identical with the material, it is often physically different, being an optical isomer of the latter, and hence producing a different physiological effect. Moreover, synthetic, or even dried or concentrated milk, although chemically and physically identical with the fresh variety, lacks the vitality and health-giving factors of fresh cow's milk.

VEGETARIAN DIET. In regard to vegetarianism, the principle of non-flesh diet is supported for reasons which will be indicated, as well as upon the general humanitarian basis. It is recognized, however, that health can be and is perfectly adequately maintained on a balanced diet which includes flesh foods in moderation, and also that it is inadvisable to advocate sudden changes in diet, no matter how strongly one may feel on the principles involved.

The reasons for this are (1) metabolic shock may result; (2) a sudden shift in diet not fully acceptable to the patient may actually prove not to be beneficial; and may result in his rejecting the whole treatment, which might have been successful if introduced to him gradually and with only minor or gradual modifications of habit.

Thus, conversely, when a patient is a convinced vegetarian on principle or of many years' standing, it is considered inadvisable to use preparations of animal origin, even when these are reduced to practically mineral condition. The reasons for this are the same as those given above, i.e. (1) psychological resistance, which is likely to create an unfavourable reaction and so defeat the purpose of the prescription; and (2) the actual fact that a body used to a non-flesh diet tends to develop fever, diarrhoea or a heavy cold in order to throw out the unaccustomed substances. Vegetarians having to go to ordinary hospitals frequently suffer in this way from the diet, as well as from doses of gland extract, liver preparations, etc., when treated as out-patients. Evidence on this point needs to be accumulated and presented to the medical profession through its own journals.[6] There is obviously no such reason against the administration of animal derivatives when patients are meat-eaters.

Many athletic records requiring great stamina have been gained and held by vegetarians, proving the adequacy of correct vegetarian diet, but ignorance, 'fads' and inadequate care do frequently result in nothing less than chronic malnutrition, and with such cases a doctor is often confronted.

This is supported by the British Medical Journal, which, in 1944, reporting a number of cases where vegetarians became ill from protein shortage, stated unequivocally that health could be maintained on a

non-flesh diet, *provided the protein intake is high enough*.[7]
One of the other dangers to vegetarians is that it is easy
to take too much starch. Also, salt is often lacking (see
page 146).

MEAT DIET IN DISEASE. The reasons for and against meat
diet in disease can be briefly put as follows:

Reasons for eating meat and fish, especially the latter,
are as follows:

(*a*) They are readily digested.
(*b*) They are often rich in vitamins A and D.
(*c*) They quickly supply energy and amino-acids.

Reasons against eating these foods, humanitarian
issues being deliberately omitted:

(*a*) Meat and fish foods putrefy readily, the process *beginning
with the death of the animal* and being only partly arrested
by cold storage. Meat may already contain (1) fatigue toxins,
due to the animals' journeys, (2) toxins due to fear, arising
from slaughter house conditions, (3) the toxins of putrefaction.[8] (*Rigor mortis*, and its passing, are the first two stages
of decomposition in any corpse.)

(*b*) Modern medical and post-surgical practice has proved the
value of eliminative non-toxin forming foods, such as fruit
juices, yeast compounds, and vegetable extracts, in fevers
and other acute conditions.

(*c*) The vitamin content can be supplied by eggs, milk, butter,
cereals, fruit and vegetables, with better effect than results
from the average meat diet.

This brief statement can be supported by scientific
evidence, but we do not consider this the proper place to
go fully into so wide a subject. The student is again
referred to the appendix for reading list.

ERRORS AND EXTREMES. There is far too much fixity of
mind in regard to diet. Superstition in regard to the need
for this or that food, or as to the benefit of special diets,
is always to be avoided. In every case the individual needs

of the patient have to be considered. The trouble is that no two dietitians agree: one wants the patient to have a mixed diet, another separates meals into those consisting mainly of protein or mainly of starch, or mainly of salad; another swears by lemon-juice, while to another it is anathema 'because it causes acid in the body'. (In fact, lemon-juice increases the *alkalinity* of the blood, and if there were *not* acid in its proper place, the stomach, the patient would be exceedingly ill.) There are some practitioners to whom glucose and sugar are deadly poisons, quite forgetting that honey, Barbadoes sugar, potatoes—even if baked in their jackets—and such like, are almost pure starch or carbohydrate of some sort, and that no carbohydrate is ever absorbed into the blood except after reduction to the form of glucose or laevulose. To others, mucus is a thing to be abhorred: yet without mucus to lubricate the system, complete stasis would result.

In short, only the scientifically and biochemically trained dietitian is really unbiased, and he is only considering the patient from one aspect. But there are two general statements which can be made about diet. One is natural foods are, in general, preferable to artificial or highly prepared foods—though the particular state of each patient needs to be considered. The other is that the patient's own appetite is often the best guide to what is appropriate, provided he has a balanced psychological outlook. The commonest cause of faddiness about food is an abnormal psychological attitude.

Salt. Some salt other than that obtained in food is necessary to the body. Wild animals seek out salt licks whenever possible, the herbivorous as well as the carnivirous. A high protein diet requires more salt because of the need for hydrochloric acid. The more perspiration is thrown off the more salt is needed. In hot climates more salt is wanted than in temperate. Lack of salt may cause muscular cramp and other symptoms. On the other hand, excess of salt is responsible for a great deal of catarrh, kidney disease in various forms, and probably certain skin complaints. Here, as elsewhere, the patient should be led towards moderation and personal experiment.

GENERAL PRINCIPLES. Having attempted in this cursory fashion to clear the field of prejudice and misapprehension we will state briefly certain principles which may aid in the selection of suitable diet for a given patient.

Dietetic Types. Much confusion exists to-day in regard to theories of dietetic treatment because variation in bodily types and the relation of this fact to dietetic needs has not been fully recognized or scientifically investigated.

There are probably four main types of diet suited to the four vital types. But the problem is complicated by the fact that individuals often do not run true to their own basic vital type, for example when a wrong diet has overloaded the system with carbohydrates, fat or protein, or when it has been starved of any necessary factor, or when metabolism is disturbed by disease conditions. An eliminative or cleansing diet or a *mild* fast (see below) is often a good preliminary treatment for such patients.

Seasonal and Occasional Diets need to be considered. The practice of recurrent fasting periods of some days, or weeks, is an ancient religious rule in many faiths and has a sound scientific basis. Special diets are desirable in hot and cold weather, for different climates, etc., but individuals with different types of bodies react very differently to temperature, and the individual must be taken as the touchstone in every instance.

When an individual is exposed to acute stress, special caution is needed and one should adhere all the more strictly to whatever diet has been found the most suitable. Some require more food when tired; with others, the digestion fails immediately with fatigue, and a light invalid diet is essential.

SPECIAL DIETS FOR DISEASE CONDITIONS. Feverish conditions in acute diseases are, in the absence of signs of collapse, an indication of the need for eliminative diet. Sub-normal temperatures and other signs of exhaustion naturally call for stimulating and energizing foods.

Convalescent cases have special needs, and certain chronic disorders require special dietaries. Each of these points will be dealt with below.

Fasting,[9] so much advocated in some circles, may be of value when a patient is overfed and his body clogged with unwanted food products. But it can be extremely dangerous and bring about serious physical and psychological collapse. It should be used only with the greatest circumspection.

Partial Fasting is in general a good thing in toxic conditions and is much safer than a complete fast. The bowels should be kept open by irrigation or simple laxative.

Partial fasts on fruit juices, etc., and eliminative treatment are very useful in special diseases.

Diet in Acute Disease, eliminative:

High fluid intake is very important. Hence, the patient should drink all the non-alcoholic liquid he reasonably can, hot or cold according to taste.

Fruit juices, especially orange, lemon, lime, tomato, grapefruit. Honey or some other form of glucose may be added if desired, and is especially valuable for children.

Vegetable soups either strained or with fibrous matter: the fibrous material assists the action of the bowels and so facilitates the elimination of poisonous waste. A useful broth is made from carrot and onion alone; or with water in which cabbage, turnips, etc., have been boiled *without salt*, to which a yeast extract such as Marmite is then added. The proportion of various mineral salts in these vegetables can be found in Bainbridge.[10] For example, turnips have a high potash content. Starchy vegetables should be eliminated as a rule.

Green vegetables or salad. Some practitioners allow these even during fever if the patient feels the need of solid food.

Barley water is very soothing, but is very starchy. Marmite is better for those who prefer salty tastes (see below).

Tomato and carrot juice have the active principle of carotene and some iron and magnesium and are very excellent tonic foods for some digestive troubles, nervous exhaustion, and other complaints involving nervous disorders. Carrot juice can be extracted by squeezing a finely-grated carrot in a strong cloth, a good-sized carrot yielding enough for one feeding, i.e. two tablespoons of juice. Can be administered with hot milk, or hot Marmite, or added vegetable juices. *Should not be boiled.*

Slippery Elm food reduces alimentary inflammation as well as being nourishing. Excellent in gastric ulcer, acute colitis, etc.

Marmite, Yeastrel and similar vegetable preparations have as basis a yeast extract, and hence are rich in Vitamin B.

Grape juice, fresh or bottled, contains iron and grape sugar (glucose). A little lemon juice added makes it more palatable for some people.

Agar-agar broth and jellies, flavoured with Marmite or fruit flavours. Non-toxin-forming, with high iodine content; more nourishing than meat broths.

Broth of simmered haricot beans with onion juice, strained.

Preparations containing irradiated ergosterol, etc.

Usual milk foods when assimilable, and in moderation.

New-laid eggs contain proteins, fats, vitamins A and D, and assimilably phosphorus and sulphur.

Convalescent Diets are ably treated in a small pamphlet issued by the London Vegetarian Society and called *Vegetarian Diet for Invalids.*[11] This gives many suggestions for a light diet of vitamin-containing foods.

HYDROTHERAPY. Water is a natural cleanser and healer, and has been used from earliest times as a healing agent. It feeds and eases the vital body. When actually cleansing the physical body, i.e. in baths and irrigations, water relieves congestion in the vital body as well as in the physical tissues. Relief given by medical baths is largely due to reactions in the vital aura and to conditions brought about in the body through these reactions. Perspiration and other phenomena of the dense physical cells resulting from these treatments are often induced by a loosening of the vital structures and the throwing out of poison at a subtle level which necessitates corresponding changes in the physical cell tissues. Special table waters are useful for their medicinal properties as well as for the effect of the extra fluid taken. Distilled water has sometimes been prescribed for drinking purposes in order to absorb waste matter, especially in rheumatism. Being practically free from all mineral content it is a very forceful solvent, and is liable to dissolve substances which may be harmful from the vessel that contains it. It is also very insipid unless fully aerated by shaking with air. It can give violent reactions by upsetting the previous chemical balance of the body, and should be taken only in small quantities at first. It is very doubtful whether it has any advantage over ordinary tap water.

Most people do not drink enough water during the twenty-four hours, but types vary in their needs. The amount of fluid taken daily needs to be watched and determined by each individual. Indian yogis and nature-cure practitioners have proved that life can be sustained for long periods on water alone, hence it would seem that a far lighter diet is feasible if ample fresh water is taken.

INTERNAL TREATMENTS. Irrigation of the colon and vaginal douching are very old cleansing treatments, and still of value in special cases to-day. Although it is occasionally necessary to give these treatments two or three times a week to offset acute conditions, constant washing of the inner membranes is obviously abnormal, and ends by weakening their capacity to do their proper work. It is by no means a natural method, as naturopaths would have us believe. Animals, if they require purgation, use the truly rational means and eat herbs and grass. Artificial irrigation is also psychologically undesirable, as it tends to fix the attention upon functions that should be automatic, and to revive early sensory experiences which should have lost their importance in adult life. Diet, massage, osteopathy, suggestion, etc., should be employed to avoid the necessity of repeated enemas.

BATHS of various kinds are useful, both for cleansing and tonic treatments.[12] Certain practitioners use Epsom salt, sea salt, and other saline baths, as well as baths of camphor, eucalyptus and pine. The uses of sea salt need to be emphasized. It is a mixture of various salts and contains the iodides and chlorides of many of the metallic elements in varying proportions; it is tonic in effect and can be used in hot or cold baths and in compresses. The well-known mustard bath serves a useful purpose at times.

COMPRESSES AND PACKS are too little used in modern medicine. High fevers can at times be quickly reduced by cold packs[13] or tepid sponging, preferably the latter, because of the possibility of shock from the cold. Local packs, hot or cold, are useful in many disorders. Certain herbal tinctures, such as arnica, calendula, hamamelis, etc., added to the water for packs, give excellent results in suitable cases.

ELECTROTHERAPY, DIATHERMY, AND RAY-THERAPY. The vital body supplies a key to many otherwise puzzling reactions in all these treatments. Clairvoyant investigation has shown that all electrical heat, light, and colour treatments act directly upon the vital body, and that the benefit received does not depend so much as has been supposed upon the penetration of the rays within the body.

Not every person can take electric or ray treatment easily, and reactions to them vary. Here are some brief statements describing reactions of various vital types. An *unstable vital body* as a rule is more shattered than helped by them. On the other hand, the *dense* type benefits from such kind of treatments, and on occasion the other three types also. A physician who observes and respects his patients' reactions to these treatments will soon distinguish the main types. Patients who have *over-tense vital bodies* are often classed as allergic because of their reactions to ray treatments. They are easily over-stimulated, and even shattered, by an apparently short dose of ultra-violet light or heat, whereas a *stable, dense and congested vital body* frequently benefits from comparatively large doses. The *bland and fluid types* vary in their reactions: if congested, they respond well to *gentle* treatment; but when somewhat unbalanced emotionally, the vital body is easily dislocated by light or heat. Sensitive chakras can become blocked or over-expanded and local pain will then appear in unexpected areas.

The following very rough generalizations may be used for checking personal observations:

INFRA-RED: Releases vital congestions and throws out toxins.

ULTRA-VIOLET: Expands the vital body, but easily over-expands it, and some leakage of vitality is likely to occur. This, of course, applies equally to strong natural sunlight.

TREATMENTS WITH GALVANIC BATTERY: Shorten the vital radiations. In some people they curl the outer edges of these and are then contra-indicated.

DIATHERMY: Conditions stimulated superficially by infra-red rays are induced deep within the vital body.

ABRAMS TREATMENTS: (Now almost defunct), shake out heavy, stagnant matter in the 'ribbon', but do not alter the outer aura much. Some remarkable and otherwise unaccountable cures have been produced by this method.

X-RAY AND RADIUM TREATMENTS: The fabric of the vital body becomes perished and brittle like a silk lampshade near a hot bulb. Thus a hole is easily made, which then results in necrosis and ulceration of the dense tissues. The disease condition may thus be destroyed, and if the general vitality of the patient is sufficient to leap the gap formed and gradually to replace the destroyed vital fabric the patient recovers, but if the general stamina is unable to replace the material thrown out the whole vital body deteriorates by leakage through the gap formed. The recuperative power of the vital body as a whole is the important factor. (Compare granulation of physical tissue.)

COLOURED LIGHT TREATMENTS. In the latter part of the nineteenth century there was great interest in the healing power of colour, and experiments were made in many countries, notably on the effect of sunlight passed through coloured glass. It was soon found that the sunlight itself was the potent agent and interest in colour treatments faded as modern ideas of ventilation, etc., developed. From time to time, however, experiments have been made with colour in relation to disease conditions of mind and body. Red light has been used in connection with the treatment of smallpox. Experiments were undertaken at Guy's Hospital upon the effect of colour in the treatment of cancer.[14] Dr. J. Dodson Hessey has given a clear description of various forms of colour treatment.[15]

Members of the group responsible for the present book have also used various forms of colour treatment over a period of years. Since the findings were arrived at independently, but accord with the results claimed by both Babbitt and Hessey, we give them in brief.

> BLACK—absence of colour—is very depressing if worn consistently, but it is stabilizing for certain florid, loose-knit types, usually etheric types 2 or 4.
>
> BLUE is astringent; it raises blood pressure, steadies excitable people, but can be depressing to the sluggish or flabby.
>
> YELLOW stimulates the cerebro-spinal system and eliminates certain kinds of inflammation.
>
> GREEN usually lowers blood pressure. Generally relieves pain, but makes certain people 'nervy'.
>
> ROSE is expansive and gently stimulating, but often too dissipative for loosely-knit etheric bodies, such as etheric type 2.
>
> ORANGE-RED is very stimulating and irritating and not good to use on very sensitive people.
>
> VIOLET is a difficult colour to use. It is healing for a few people, but easily produces a curiously unbalanced condition which is sometimes mistaken for increased vital activity.

It is difficult to obtain a beam of pure colour, and variations in the use of colour by practitioners, and in the results reported, may well be due to variations in the glass or other colour filters used. Our workers preferred the Kodak Colour Filters, when obtainable, or solutions of chemicals in thin glass tanks. There is also a very large psychological factor involved in the effect of the colour itself, as well as in the situation created during the treatment, for which sufficient allowance is not always made. Colour affects all the bodies to some extent, the reaction at the psychological level often being the stronger. For example, the effect of a colour wave-length upon the vital field of a patient's body can easily be offset by the personal like or dislike of the given colour, or the emotional reaction to the treatment as a whole.

While there is no doubt that treatments with coloured light may have an ultimate healing effect on the physical body, if skilfully administered, they can also act as stimulus to suggestive treatment, and the latter is often the most important element in the result. With so many factors involved, claims made for the benefits of colour treatments *per se*, and for cures effected wholly by this medium, should be viewed with caution.

VITAL MAGNETIC HEALING. This is the age-old method of healing 'by the laying on of hands'. Through it the healer pours vitality into a sick person's vital body, and so restores in him the normal flow of prāna, or vital energy. The results may be temporary or permanent, varying according to circumstances which are fully described in a special transaction dealing with the subject.[16]

The treatment varies from a simple laying on of hands and an act of faith, to highly specialized passes given by a trained student. Frequently vitality is given to patients by doctors unconsciously during interviews or examinations, and often in bedside visits. Masseuses often give some vitality to patients, both consciously and unconsciously.

The treatment has a direct effect upon the vital body, cleansing, feeding and readjusting it, but the effect of the treatment is very much limited by the personal reactions of the patient, since these also directly influence his vital body. Obviously the conditions of the dense physical body need to be dealt with at their own level at the same time, e.g. it is useless to employ vital passes to clean up the vital structures associated with toxic intestines when what is really wanted is a high colonic irrigation or, more simply, a brisk purge.

The most effective uses of magnetic healing are for:

1. Conditions of shock, both physical and psychological, as it can ease the chakras and relieve strain in the vital body.
2. Post-surgical cases, maternity work, etc., for the same reason.
3. In cases needing gradual building up, e.g. convalescence, exhaustion, etc., where a mild, steady pressure towards health gradually brings the patient back to his normal condition.

There are real dangers in giving the treatment, as a doctor or nurse can be too much drawn upon by patients who are unconscious vampires, i.e. who prefer to live on other people's vitality rather than specialize their own. As the subject has been amply treated in the published transaction cited above, this section has been curtailed.

IV. PHARMACEUTICAL PREPARATIONS

GENERAL REMARKS. Owing to the misuse of drugs there is a general tendency on the part of certain modern healers to deny the usefulness of any pharmaceutical preparation. Yet medicines have their place in the scheme of things, and not only assist cure, but may save patients much unnecessary suffering.

Before discussing the properties of some of these substances in detail, it is essential to have a perfectly clear conception of their nature. Pharmaceutical preparations, or drugs as they are often called, consist of two main groups and one smaller group. The vast majority of these remedies are found in the first two classifications, which consist of (1) materials obtained from the plant world by making dry or liquid extracts or solutions, and sometimes simply by powdering a part of the plant when dry. (2) Substances prepared from the mineral kingdom. (3) There is also a small group of substances, like cod-liver oil and thyroid gland extract, which are obtained from the animal world. (4) The sulphonamides, penicillin, etc. These actually fall under headings (1) and (2) above, but will be considered separately. (See page 169).

We should like to draw attention at this point to a fallacy, which it is by no means unusual to hear expressed, concerning the harmlessness of 'herbal remedies'. The fact is that the most highly potent and deadly poisonous drugs used in pharmacy, such as opium, cocaine, aconite, belladonna, and nux vomica, to mention only a few, are all herbal remedies. The common mineral poisons arsenic and mercury are considerably less toxic than a number of the herbal substances used in medicine. Herbal remedies are by no means always harmless nor to be considered merely as additional food.

SEDATIVES AND EMERGENCY TREATMENT. In spite of the deadening effect of sedatives upon the vital structures and functions, there are times when narcotics such as morphine and cocaine are of the greatest value in that they prevent and relieve shock and pain. This is often the case after serious accidents, especially if amputations have to be performed hurriedly. In a similar way, the chemicals used as anæsthetics are of inestimable benefit to mankind in surgery and midwifery. And, again, it often happens that the only way of saving a person's life in cases of poisoning is to give large doses of an antidote which may itself be a poison.

The bromides and barbiturates belong to another group of sedative drugs which, although harmful when used habitually, are of great value in cases of insomnia due to shock or worry or for uncontrollable tempers in children due to excessive irritability of the general nervous system. A short treatment with small doses of one of the members of this group will often bring the patient into a state of mind which is capable of responding to methods of re-education or of psychotherapy, when, without the sedative, this would not have been possible. Cases of epilepsy which have been uninfluenced by any of the other treatments mentioned in this book can be greatly alleviated by certain barbituric acid derivatives; fits occurring three or four times a week disappearing entirely.

Certain people also object categorically to the use of hypodermic injections, but there are emergencies, as in cases of accident or unconsciousness, when the hypodermic injection of a drug will stimulate respiration or a failing heart, or cause vomiting of poisonous material lying in the stomach, and in this way save the patient's life. So, although the use of a hypodermic syringe as a routine measure of treatment is to be deprecated, instances occur when its use is essential or, at least, a better way of dealing with matters than the oral route.

There is also a group of complex diseases where nothing seems to equal the administration of certain animal preparations. Very severe cases of asthmatic paroxysms, for example, can be relieved by subcutaneous injection of adrenalin, a 1 - 1,000 solution, and death from heart strain prevented as a result, while cases of myxoedema frequently respond remarkably well to adequate doses of dried thyroid gland when given by the mouth.

REMEDIES IN COMMON AILMENTS. So far we have dealt with cases needing drastic or emergency treatment, for which there seems to be no remedy other than a pharmaceutical one. Besides these, there is a large group of common ailments in the treatment of which pharmaceutical remedies are of greater service than are other methods. Such remedies need not be used exclusively, but it can be said that unless allopathic drugs are used in these cases patients either recover more slowly or not completely.

A few illustrations only will be given: Tertiary syphilitic conditions of any part of the body (Pencillin); intestinal parasites (Male Fern, Gentian Violet, etc.), acute rheumatism (Sodii Salicyl.); simple goitre (Iodine); dysentery, colitis, cholera (Kaolin), Malaria (Paludrine, Mepacrine, Quinine); angina pectoris, and raised blood pressure (Nitrites); deficiency of gastric secretion (HCl.); gastric ulcers (Magnesia, Calc. Carb., Bis. Carb.); cystitis (Pot. Cit., Hyoscy.); dry, ineffective, painful cough of phthisis (Diamorphine, Codeine); dry bronchitis (Ipec., Amm. Chlor., Pot. Bicarb.); auricular fibrillation (Digitalis).

This section has been written in moderate detail, not because it is regarded as the most important section of the book but in order to emphasize the view that *there is no panacea for the curing of disease*. The claims of any particular system of medication need clear and careful analysis, not only in terms of successes but by a statistical comparison of successes and failures. Every system claims results. The doubtful matter is whether these are, in fact, any better than those of other systems. All must be considered with an open mind, and the best remedy, or combination of remedies, selected for the treatment of the individual case.

HOMOEOPATHY. In the past homoeopathic remedies have often been ridiculed because of the minute quantity of any remedy given as a dose. The homoeopathic position with regard to this now receives support in the light of recent work on catalysts, vitamins, etc., wherein science has recognized that the effect of a certain given substance is out of all proportion to the quantity present in the blood stream or to the size of the particles. Further, the significance of extremely minute amounts of chemical substances for plant growth has recently been carefully studied. Microscopic traces of these substances in the soil have geen found to be sufficient to promote growth, while in their absence the plants are weak and retarded. In connection with animal life it has been found that iron administered for anaemia proves effective only in the presence of minute traces of copper,[17] and many other remedies work best when there are in them traces of other substances.

For the general theory and practice of homoeopathy readers are referred to the textbooks.[18] Here we shall, as before, deal only with points which are of special significance in relation to the views we are presenting.

POTENCIES. Homoeopathic remedies act directly on the vital body, the process of 'potentization', which is the technical name for the preparation of homoeopathic remedies, in some way altering the characteristics of the substance. They do not replace absent chemical material. The *higher* the potency the more powerful may be its effect. The high potency remedy is like a bullet shot from a high velocity rifle. If it hits, it hits very hard, but it is more easy to miss when using this than when using a shot-gun, the latter being an equivalent for the *lower* potency. Also a high potency remedy may miss its effect, no matter how direct the aim, by being over-specific and over-subtle, and therefore failing to affect a patient who might react powerfully to a lower potency or to a massive dose.

High potencies work especially on the two subtlest radiations of the vital body, certain others (30 and lower) affect the heavier ethers, and the lowest potencies affect the double itself (see page 36).

TISSUE SALTS. Certain mineral salts to which the title *Tissue Salts* has been given by some practitioners, are regarded as of special importance for normal metabolism, and small doses of these particular salts, as well as others, are given as tonics.[19] Yet remedies given in infinitesimal doses cannot actually replace mineral losses from the body in the same way that administration of the non-potentized mineral salts replaces them. As this point is a matter of some controversy we will attempt to make our position clear.

It is true that the total amount of the mineral salts required by the body is small, and that when these salts are administered in bulk, as a remedy, by far the greater part is excreted in the urine. It has also been found, as we have said, that the giving of mineral elements that have passed through the vegetable kingdom is more effective than the administration of pure inorganic salts from the earth, or prepared in the laboratory, because some subtle change occurs in the vital structure of these salts as a result of their incorporation in living tissues. Having been thus incorporated they are more readily assimilable by the human body and through a carefully planned diet including unfired foods, carrot juice, orange juice, etc., it is possible to supply in full the mineral salts required by the body in inorganic form. Yet when something goes wrong with the metabolic processes themselves the salts supplied even in this form are frequently not utilized.

Homoeopathic remedies affect such conditions by acting directly upon the process of metabolism from the vital level. A person who is lacking in calcium does not always need a homoeopathic remedy containing calcium, but rather a remedy determined by the nature of his symptoms and temperament, which so influences metabolism as to allow him to utilize the calcium in his food. In support of this, one can cite the well-known fact that massive doses of calcium may be administered to such a patient without beneficial result. What is needed is stimulation of his capacity to deal with his calcium problem in the ordinary processes of digestion. The small doses of Tissue Salts appear to act simply as low potency homoeopathic remedies and have no proved connection with any possible deficiency of the salt administered as a remedy.

PRESCRIPTION. On reading literature about homoeopathy one often finds a reference to seeing the 'typical sulphur patient' as he walks into the room, so that it would seem that the homoeopath has virtually prescribed before he has heard the details of the patient's complaint. Similarly, it has been found that a patient may not respond to a series of drugs which appear to be indicated by the symptoms, and only when the practitioner throws theory to the winds and gives a drug which has haunted the background of his mind do the patient's symptoms abate. This strongly suggests that the successful practice of homoeopathy demands, more than do most other treatments, the intuitive approach.

The range at which homoeopathic remedies work is partly accountable for this fact. As in our view homoeopathic remedies act directly upon the vital body it follows that there is a two-fold problem in administration: (1) There is the effect of the remedy upon the vital matrix itself, which involves a consideration of the vital type and static vital conditions. (2) As the capacity of the vital body to react to a remedy is also determined by the psychological state of the patient, which conditions the flow and balance of the higher prānas, psychological symptoms are of the utmost significance when prescribing homoeopathic remedies, especially in chronic diseases.

Practitioners are often puzzled by a drug failing to affect a patient who apparently gives clear indications of the need for it. This may easily be due to hidden psychological symptoms or to the quality of the vital type; e.g. arnica is a remedy which often acts well for strains, sprains and bruises, but it has been known to fail completely in certain individuals with a vital body of type 4.

Only experience can assist the general practitioner in learning to discern the remedies demanded by the immediate conditions. When the general quality of the usual remedies has been realized, together with their action as *homoeopathic entities*, it is often safe to act on a purely intuitive or even an apparently instinctual impulse. Some psychometric or psychological link at the vital level seems to be made between the patient and the remedy, and this asserts itself in the doctor as the impulse to prescribe that particular drug. This happens, of course, with all treatments, but seems particularly active in connection with homoeopathy because of the range at which it works For the same reasons, the pendulum or divining rod, the Boyd-Abrams diagnostic machine, the Pathoclast and other 'emanometers' are sometimes useful in ascertaining the correct homoeopathic remedy to prescribe.[20]

The drawbacks to homoeopathic treatments are, roughly, (1) that some patients have more confidence in a bottle of medicine, i.e. in a substantial and conventional dose, than in 'drops' or minute quantities; (2) that some vital and physical bodies are too dense or too rigid to give adequate response to homoeopathy; (3) that psycho-

L

logical factors actually rule the vital condition, hence whenever the treatment is aimed mainly at physical or vital symptoms, a resistant or confused psyche can defeat it more easily than it can the massive dose.

The advantages, in the same order, again roughly stated, are: (1) that many people have lost confidence in allopathic treatments; (2) that an increasing number of people to-day have highly sensitive vital and physical bodies and need very delicate dosing, free from the tendency to secondary reactions due to drug residues—this being particularly true for patients with psychic temperaments, neurotics and mental cases; (3) that the homoeopath takes into account the psychological type of his patient and deals as much with the psychic as with the vital and dense physical bodies, hence his diagnosis is more complete and treatment is more likely to be profoundly curative.

Homoeopathy, when rightly understood, can be effective in overcoming constitutional weaknesses in children and sensitives, but patience and flexibility in the use of cleansing and tonic remedies are needed for this work.

While homoeopathic treatment is used exclusively by some general practitioners, persons usually found to be most suited for homoeopathy are children, convalescents, elderly fragile people, and those using special diets which tend to purify the body; psychics and sensitives of all sorts; allergic types and chronic invalids, particularly when these have been overdosed or mishandled by other methods of medical or surgical treatment. The above groups are obviously composed of those in whom vital and psychological reactions are a dominant factor in matters of health and hence should be given an equal or even greater significance than the dense physical body and its symptoms.

It is worth recording the fact that Hahnemann and his followers have repeatedly emphasized the principle which we have considered to be fundamental, namely that it is the patient and not the symptoms that should be treated. This principle is summed up in the well-known homoeopathic aphorism, *There are no diseases, but sick people.*[21]

TREATMENTS WITH GLAND EXTRACTS. There are on the market many preparations, often widely advertised, derived from the endocrine glands of animals, and also many synthetic drugs used as substitutes for glandular secretions.

We have stated earlier that the chakras of the vital and subtler bodies influence the areas in which the endocrine glands are placed. (See table, page 41.) The glands seem to act as the chief focal points through which certain qualities of the psyche impinge upon the metabolism of the physical body. For example, certain influences pour through the throat chakram[22] from the mental, astral and vital levels, and according to the healthy or unhealthy condition of the psyche, affect the thyroid and parathyroid glands. Following on unbalance of these glands, thus caused, the physical functions affected by their hormones, such as calcium metabolism in the case of parathyroid unbalance, become deranged.

The whole system of correspondences set forth in Chapter V (page 121) should be reviewed as a background for these statements, as well as the relationship of the subtle bodies to the vital matrix, and the vital body as a whole to the physical.

Thus it follows that administration of gland extract does not get to the root of the trouble, but is a substitute for mal-function only. That the balance of metabolism is *at times* improved by this substitution cannot be denied, but there are risks involved.

While admitting in certain striking cases the administration of gland extract has apparently been justified by the results, these cases are fewer than literature on the subject would lead us to believe. Let us agree that with some morons, with certain types of depressed and suicidal mental cases, and in cases where surgical removal of the glands has deprived the patient altogether of normal secretions of a given type, administration of a selected gland extract may be indicated. For these and other obvious deficiencies, if the patient is not a vegetarian and has no scruples about taking these medicines, it may be necessary to prescribe simple preparations of a given gland extract, such as thyroid, pituitrin, etc. Even in the cases just defined it should be recognized that this is a substitutional treatment and does not reach the cause of the disease.

The tendency to prescribe gland treatment too hastily and without positive indications is to be deprecated, and this for the following reasons:

1. In most cases so little is known about the intricacies of the psycho-physical reactions of these glands that it is impossible to prescribe with any certainty. While obtuse and materialistic natures may not be harmed by the disturbance of normal relationship inevitably caused through substituting an external dose for an internal secretion, sensitive types frequently give disquieting reactions to gland treatment, showing that such derangement of function does occur.

2. Other remedies, which are sometimes equally or more efficacious, should be tried first. Many homoeopathic remedies such as phosphorus, calcium phosphate, thuja, etc., when effective on the patient, as a whole, must automatically affect the endocrine system.

3. The use of poly-glandular mixtures, administered on the chance of hitting off the right combination of stimuli to produce normal metabolism is crude and, in view of other disadvantages, undesirable.

4. In sensitive patients the root-trouble is probably psychological. They need relaxation, re-education and rest, or at most a dose of the right medicine, rather than complicated physical treatments.

5. Clairvoyant observation has shown that even where the physical conditions have improved under gland treatment, e.g. obesity reduced by thyroid extract, the nervous

function nevertheless sometimes tends to deteriorate and the higher functions of consciousness to be inhibited through the blocking of the active vital centre in the chakras concerned. This is particularly true of the head and throat chakras. While such reactions may be merely an effect of overdosage, it is admittedly difficult to gauge exactly the best amount to give to any particular patient.

GLAND TREATMENT IN PREGNANCY AND LABOUR. Gland extract is rarely advocated in pregnancy.

If the right psychological attitude can be instilled during pregnancy, the relaxation of pelvic nerves and muscles cultivated, and a rightly balanced diet taken, labour should be a natural process, and endocrine treatment is then unnecessary.[23] But repeated miscarriage or sterility have often been prevented or cured by the use of suitable preparations of endocrine extracts.

GLAND DEFICIENCY. In dealing with diseases due to deficiency of glandular secretions, many doctors feel that by administering gland extract they are affecting the root or cause of the disease, but this is not the case, for the causes of glandular disturbance itself are, as we have shown, psychological. The administration of the extract is actually dealing with symptoms of the disease rather than with its cause.

The subject, as all know, is a very complicated one. In general, glandular preparations, even when pure, should only be used in self-evident cases and as a last resort, when other methods (including expert psychological treatment) of stimulating the glands to normal activity or of supplying the deficiency, have failed. This type of treatment is not in line with the basic principles of this book, as it is substitutional and symptomatic; it usually does work for the body instead of releasing the psychophysical energies necessary to establish a normal and self-sustaining metabolism. It does not touch the karmic or psychological causes of disharmony, and these probably underlie all causes of disturbance in the endocrine system. Although many patients will be resistant to this idea, to secure real endocrine balance the psychological problem underlying glandular dysfunction needs to be dealt with at its own level. All else is palliation, not cure.

EXTERNAL APPLICATIONS. These may be divided into four main groups:

(1) Those that promote the excretion of poisonous substances, e.g. anhydrous magnesium sulphate in glycerine.
(2) Those that, by their astringent action, lessen excretion from the skin, e.g. zinc compounds, alum, tannic acid, certain aniline dyes.
(3) Counter-irritants, e.g. turpentine, wet and dry heat, most liniments, iodine.
(4) Those that relieve pain and irritation, e.g. winter-green, menthol, cocaine.

Applications in group (1) are used in acute septic conditions. This at once leads to an increased activity of the septic area, which, to the untrained eye, might seem detrimental but as it is essential that localized sepsis be eliminated before the skin is allowed to heal, the treatment is perfectly rational as, for example, in the case of boils and carbuncles.

Applications from the second group are of pre-eminent importance where destruction of tissue has occurred, as in burns. If applied at once, before secondary sepsis has set in, they will usually succeed in forming a protective, artificial covering for the whole of the area concerned, and thus prevent sepsis occurring. They also prevent vital leakage and stop the absorption of poisons from the destroyed tissue. In this respect, the free application of Triple Dye or tannic acid to serious burns is an excellent example of how the simple, coagulating action of an ordinary chemical can prevent serious toxaemia or dehydration and save life where a healing method involving a more subtle or more delicate physiological reaction would fail. In mild burns, where the skin is unbroken, the mere application of a thin film of vaseline will often ease the pain by preventing vital leakage.

It is important to have a clear idea as to what is happening in the skin when dealing with a diseased skin condition, and never to use an astringent where an eliminant is necessary. When an eczema is due to an allergic condition of the skin, sedative or astringent applications may be indicated, but it is found that superficial eruptions and rashes often indicate the elimination of poison through the skin, and if a medicament is applied which merely cures the rash it may be pushing back into the system poisons that the body is trying to throw off. The curing of such eczema by means of an astringent ointment may therefore cause a serious discharge from some other part of the body, or the poisoning of an excretory organ by overtaxing it.[24] In such cases, if the eczematous patient is given general eliminative treatment, with an increase of vitamins and tissue-cleansing foods while decreasing the intake of excessive salt and protein—which tax the organs of excretion—it will often be found that the patient's general health will improve and the eczematous rash will disappear.

In treating skin conditions one must distinguish clearly between a localized condition, such as bite, burn, abscess, scabies, and a more generalized dyscrasia such as causes eczema, psoriasis or urticaria. It is better not to treat the latter by local application except to relieve irritation or, occasionally, with eliminative applications to provoke the discharge of toxins. Diet, constitutional medicines, exercise, psychotherapy or remedial measures including general hygiene, are more successful for the general conditions.

In cases where local applications are indicated it is necessary in making a choice to distinguish between the more and the less active drugs. Tannic acid becomes inert upon application to the skin. Its action is therefore strictly local, while iodine and picric acid, even when so applied, remain active, may be absorbed into the system, and may even damage the vital body very severely. There are useful non-poisonous substitutes for iodine and the cresol and carbolic groups of antiseptics, all of which are definitely detrimental to the vital body since they are destructive to vital tissues. They destroy far more than the toxic substances they are used to attack. Antiseptics which are non-toxic (e.g. Dettol) or only slightly so (e.g. flavine) are undoubtedly to be preferred, and better results will occur through their routine use.

The essential oils and balsams have stimulating as well as antiseptic properties, and are much to be preferred for highly sensitive types. Again, certain homoeopathic remedies may be mentioned here, such as calendula and urtica urens.

Local anaesthetics such as cocaine derivatives may be employed in emergency, but their use should not be prolonged and should be avoided whenever possible because of their disturbing effect upon vital structures.

Personal idiosyncrasies need to be carefully observed, both in regard to reactions to medicaments and in regard to the psychological background from which all skin as well as other physical difficulties arise.

Persistent skin eruptions are closely allied to conditions in the vital skin, and as this responds to the subtle reactions of the psyche to its environment, the psychological state of a patient suffering from recurrent skin trouble is of the utmost importance. Skin eruptions often have a definite predilection for certain areas of the body; hence the correspondence of the part of the body affected to a particular psychological state, sometimes, though not always, gives a useful clue to the underlying psychological problem. Persistent disturbances of the condition of the skin are often difficult and disappointing to treat because the causes of chronic skin trouble lie so deep. Needless to say, in cases where the psychological difficulty is deep-rooted, the patient will be entirely unaware of it, and a statement on the part of the doctor that such a difficulty exists may do more harm than good. If the patient can himself be induced to discover the psychological irritant and to make some adaptation to it, a permanent cure is probable, but the doctor will often be forced to compromise and use palliatives.

Group three: members of this group are used when there is deep-seated congestion of some kind causing circulatory and vital stagnation. By stimulating the nerve-endings in the skin they bring about an increased superficial vascularity, and thus relieve the congestion at deeper levels. For this reason, counter-irritants often act as members of the first group and cause the elimination of poisons via the skin; hence the use of poultices and hot fomentations in the treatment of abscesses or in catarrhal conditions of the lungs.

Group four: these substances are used when the lesion in the skin is very painful or greatly irritating and the condition is not relieved in the early stages by the curative treatment outlined above. Local sedatives are valuable, since by deadening the sensitiveness of the nerve-endings in the skin, the patient is able to rest, and his normal recuperative forces are thus enabled to do their work unimpeded.

Chemotherapy

As repeatedly pointed out elsewhere in this book, the fundamental causes of disease are subtle and usually deep-seated. The prime cause is not to be found in such a simple thing as chance infection by a germ. Nevertheless, micro-organisms often play an important part in the chain of events we call disease, and especially in acute conditions such as pneumonia, colds and septicaemia. They seem to act as a precipitating factor where the other causes necessary are present, and when the disease is established, their activity gives rise to effects we should consider secondary, but which nevertheless add very much to the ill health of the patient, and may even be the cause of his death. For a long time, therefore, scientists have been seeking for substances which, if taken into the patient's system, would either destroy or prevent the growth of the organisms associated with a specific disease without killing the patient also, and preferably with a minimum of toxic effect on him.

Certain chemical substances have now been found, belonging to the sulphonamide group, which have these properties to a limited extent. By stopping the growth of organisms connected with such ailments as puerperal fever, pneumonia, cerebro-spinal meningitis, erysipelas and certain other diseases with a high mortality, they slow down the destructive process, giving the body time to build up its own healing resources, thereby bringing about a cure where, in the past, the very rapidity of the progress of the infection would have terminated fatally before the body had had time to react properly. The drugs themselves do not cure the disease, but remove the agent that stands in the way of the cure.

Unfortunately, the drugs themselves are by no means harmless and tend to cause ill health, though, when wisely administered, these side-effects are less serious than the ills they are used to check. For this reason, they should only be given by experts, in properly chosen cases, and not tried arbitrarily as is so often done, perhaps under pressure from a patient who has read sensational articles in the newspapers, and thinks he is being deprived of something if the doctor does not immediately send him a supply of 'M. and B.' if he has a cold or sore throat.

Penicillin, derived from a lowly plant of the mould family, is another such substance. It not only inhibits many of the sulphonamide-sensitive organisms, but a number of others as well. Moreover, it is far less poisonous to human beings than the sulphonamides. In early days pencillin had the disadvantage of having to be injected under the skin at frequent intervals, however there are now modified forms of penicillin, as well as other antibiotics, which in suitable cases can be taken by mouth, but like the sulphonamides they should only be taken under expert guidance.

v. Treatment of Mental Disease

A. Physical Treatment

CONVULSION THERAPY AND PREFRONTAL LEUCOTOMY. Two treatments much in vogue at present in psychiatric circles are electrical convulsion therapy (E.C.T.) and prefrontal leucotomy.

In E.C.T., the patient is laid on a couch, electrodes are put on his temples, and he is given an electrical shock which sends him into a fit which is exactly the same to look at as the fit of epilepsy. The idea of this, which is a development from similar lines of approach where chemical substances were used, is that the shock will jerk the patient out of a depressed or anxious mental condition and restore him to normal.

In fact, it has been found that in depressive psychoses, where the patient is in a state of melancholia and cannot shake himself out of it, E.C.T. does in certain cases produce what seem to be good results. In anxiety states, the results are much more doubtful, while in derangements of the intellect such as schizophrenia or paranoia, they are practically nil. Moreover, because it saves a great deal of time and trouble, a very large number of cases are submitted to this form of treatment without any attempt being made to treat them by psychological means—i.e. to get at the root cause of the disease. This in itself is a bad principle in any form of therapy.

But there is another aspect of the matter which is that, from the psychic angle, this treatment is extremely damaging. To take the more obvious things first, there is the fact that some patients are terrified of it, and this in itself is bad. Some, however, enjoy it, and it has been suggested that this is because of the sense of complete self-surrender which is akin to the surrender of sexual orgasm. It is obvious that this too is most undesirable, just as stimulation by drugs is a poor substitute for real and natural well-being.

Further, while the convulsion is taking place, the vital body of the patient is violently shot out of the dense physical. This is a great deal more damaging even than natural epilepsy, because the latter, unpleasant as it is, is the climax of a gradual building up of forces within the individual, whereas in E.C.T. the vital structure is suddenly wrenched out and left to find its own way back, which it does with varying success. There is often great damage to the solar plexus chakram, if not to others, and many patients also complain of very poor memory after the treatment. If, as is often the case, E.C.T. is given as a 'cure' for shock such as bomb shock or psychological shock, the victim then has to be treated, not only for the original blow, but for the additional ones imposed on the already bruised personality. Thus the psychotherapist, who is the right person to deal with such cases, has a double task before him.

It needs to be realised that, even where E.C.T. jerks a person out of a phase of depression, it does not touch the real complaint, and this is why so many cases sooner or later fall back again. It is as if one had a jar of sweets which have stuck together because of damp in the jar. One jolts them up and they separate and even change their relative positions. But when one stops shaking the jar, they slowly settle down again into a solid lump. The only valid answer to the problem is to remove the moisture and dry the contents of the jar, and this cannot be done from outside.

Another thing which is done far too often even from the viewpoint of the materialistic, is prefrontal leucotomy. This consists in a surgical procedure whereby part of the prefrontal convolutions of the brain are cut off from the rest. It is used, or should be, in chronic and intractable cases of melancholia or uncontrollable bad behaviour, and is said, when the patient survives—the death-rate from the operation being extremely high—to restore the patient to a more or less normal state of behaviour. The damage to the brain is irreparable, so that once the operation is done, it can never be undone. And, invariably, the patient's level of behaviour is at a more primitive and lower level than that when he was normal. The higher functions, originality, creativeness, etc., are all more or less affected.

What this amounts to is that, because a person persists in walking on the corns of society, if one can prevent him from walking, then he can no longer tread on one's toes and he is therefore deemed cured of his disease—even though he can no longer walk at all, or if he can walk, he can only do so with difficulty.

Enough has been said to make it obvious that there is a vast difference between the people who consider psychotherapy from the point of view merely of the outer surface of the human being, that is, his behaviour in society, and those who go deeper and consider the human being as a whole, with a right to receive certain services from society as well as having a duty to his fellow men. If one belongs to the first class, then one may be justified in sacrificing the individual to society in order to save oneself time and trouble in looking after him. If one is of the other, then even if the patient has given his consent, one must see in these treatments a dangerous and almost certainly unjustifiable assault on the spiritual man.

DRUGS, PROLONGED NARCOSIS. It needs to be remembered that the majority of mental cases are of psychological origin. Physical treatments, therefore, cannot touch the root cause. But there are instances where this root cause cannot be reached because the patient is inaccessible to verbal methods of approach. In such a case, it may become necessary to use drugs if the patient is restless and noisy, or to break a vicious circle of insomnia, and restore the rhythm of sleep. This is justifiable, provided it is remembered that drugs have a deleterious effect on the vital body, and that prolonged use inevitably leads to deterioration, particularly of the subtler and higher functions of the brain.

It is thus a choice of evils: is it better to allow a manic

patient to kill himself from exhaustion due to frenzied activity, or to drug him for a few days until he quiets down and returns to relatively normal life, as many of them do after the acute crisis is over? Common-sense answers this question.

What is harmful, however, is the very common practice of glibly giving a prescription for phenobarbitone, sometimes for years on end, to a patient perfectly susceptible to psychological treatment. Bromides are also much abused. These things serve their purpose if, in the middle of a spell of over-work, they are used to give the patient relief for a time and enable him to get a second breath. But they should not be given as a routine, over long periods.

A treatment found of considerable value in wartime, when dealing with men in a state of shock due to exhaustion as well as to battle experiences, has been that of putting them to sleep for the major part of twenty-four hours, perhaps for several weeks at a time. Drugs or insulin have been used for this, the patient being fed regularly all the time. The value of this method is to rest the body and to give it a chance of rebuilding itself, which it would not do if the patient were in a constant state of restlessness due to fear or remembered horror. It was found to work well in cases treated early before the shock pattern had been fully established.

Again, one has to choose between a patient perhaps becoming temporarily insane as a result of his experiences, the lesser damage of drugs on the vital body. The drugs can eventually be dominated, whereas insanity leaves a permanent residue of damage in the patient.

B. PSYCHOTHERAPY

SUGGESTION.[25] Some form of psychological treatment is involved in the approach of every healer to his patient. The good 'bedside manner' is admittedly invaluable because it means power to use suggestion in a skilled and, of course, perfectly legitimate way. The suggestion conveyed by the healer that he really knows what to do, and is going to give help and relief, is an integral part of his treatment although it is not usually recognized as such. The power of suggestion is, after all, merely the power that one mind has to convey to another mind an idea or point of view. When the point of view conveyed is that the treatment will be successful, this relaxes psychological pressure, eases nervous tension, and so increases the flow of prāna. The free flow of vital energy enables recovery more easily to take its natural course. The candid healer admits that improvement is frequently due as much to relief induced by the healer's visit as to the remedy prescribed.

All healing by suggestion works in the manner indicated above. Certain practitioners have found it possible to rely wholly upon suggestion and to eliminate medicine. The student of eastern psychology who recognizes the activities of the unseen bodies of man can give some explanation as to how this works.

The condition known as disease, particularly chronic disease, constitutes a vicious circle, psychological cause producing physical disturbance. The circle can be broken at the physical level, temporarily, at any rate, by change of diet, exercise, medicine or other physical treatment. It can also be broken by a change of psychological state as modern psychotherapy has amply proved. *Suggestion* is a method of treatment whereby a psychological change is induced in the patient that alters his psychological attitude towards disease, and consequently alters his unconsciously-built thought-mould, the latter directly affecting the vital body and the flow of prāna. Prāna follows thought; the vital activities in the area which has been congested, distorted or exhausted, pick up the healthier quality of the new mental impulse, and a change in the vital condition results. This change may be slight, and sustained only during the practitioner's visit, or it may be deep-seated and result in substantial improvement.

It will vary according to the nature of the disease, the frequency of the visits, the patient's temperament and the amount of actual vital magnetism which the patient picks up from the doctor along with the suggestion.

In this connection there are patients of two types: those who are open to suggestion and those who are not. The nature of the suggestible patient is such that he readily receives an impression of possible improvement, reproduces this in himself both mentally and emotionally, and often makes a picture of this improvement as actually having taken place, even localizing it by imagining the diseased part of the body as more at ease. In the technique of suggestion this is the correct use of the imagination, of which M. Coué so strongly approved.

The patient who is resistant to suggestion rejects the suggestion of improvement, either mentally, emotionally or physically. If he is mentally rigid, he cannot pick up the idea readily; if he has mental-emotional complexes or withdrawals which are antagonistic to the idea of health, he shuts out at some unconscious level all idea of recovery. There are also rigid physical conditions where organic deterioration has gone so far that suggestive treatment would have to be carried on for a longer time and more intensively than is usually attempted. Miracles do, of course, occur, but these probably come under the heading of spiritual healing rather than of suggestion.

The misuse of will, of which M. Coué spoke so much, would, in our terms, be an interference constituted by fixed or over-intense desire, i.e. emotion strongly attached to a rigid mental picture. In such a case, it is mental fixity and emotional over-intensity that inhibit curative change, not the will as the eastern psychologist views it. M. Coué was entirely right in showing that any activity of such *personal* willing, i.e. the tension of personal desire, inhibits the effect of suggestive treatment. It brings into activity, at the mental-emotional level, strong restrictive tensions which at once build their counterparts in the vital body, and these vital tensions are definitely inimical to a free flow of prāna and to the desired change towards a freer and more healthy vital mould. When desire and imagination conflict, there is really a conflict of two aspects of desire, and the one with the clearer mental picture attached (i.e. most clearly or persistently imagined) will almost certainly win. If the true will is used, it can be directed to induce relaxation of mind and body, and thus can be effective in producing the calm receptivity of both requisite for effective suggestion.

Individual idiosyncrasy of the most subtle character is of as much significance in all forms of healing by suggestion as it is in diet, or in relation to reactions to light or to drugs. The very usual statement that failure to be helped by suggestion indicates a deep-seated desire to remain ill is too broad a generalization. Sometimes it does indicate this, sometimes it does not.

In our view, then, suggestion is an inevitable part of every treatment. The wise doctor studies its technique, becomes aware of its effects, and uses it as a natural expression of a genuine attitude on his part. This attitude accepts the facts that: (1) his skill is of real use in treating disease; (2) the patient's attitude to disease and recovery is an integral part of the problem; (3) the reactions of mind and body are both improved by reasonable optimism; (4) the establishment of a healing flow of life in the patient is assisted by confidence in the doctor as well as by the actual vitality conveyed at times by personal contact or conscious magnetic treatment. Sincerity on the part of the doctor in regard to all these points will enable him to use suggestion in a legitimate fashion.

ANALYTICAL THERAPY. The doctor who takes a good medical and personal history of his patient in a friendly manner has performed a useful piece of psychotherapy, in that he has encouraged the patient to relieve his mind and to speak freely of difficult matters, and in that he has established a relationship of confidence and trust between the patient and himself.

There is an actual therapeutic value in the mere fact of

M

the patient being able to speak freely about himself to another person who receives what is said impersonally and yet with understanding. The sharing of a painful secret *ipso facto* relieves strain and diminishes its burden and hence its disease-creating potentiality.

Yet it is a great mistake to suppose that conversations of a confidential nature between doctor and patient constitute analysis. The technique of analysis is of a highly specialized nature for which the general practitioner who is unanalysed is as little equipped as he would be to administer a highly-specialized sanatorium treatment. We feel that this point should be stressed, as much harm is done by genuinely well-intentioned people who do not realize the technical qualifications needed to conduct a successful analysis. There are many well-meaning but untrained would-be psychotherapists who may do superficial good, but who are quite unfit to deal with serious cases. The only school of training for deep analysis is to go through analysis oneself. No analyst can deal adequately with a problem of which he himself has not had conscious experience and which he has not dealt with in himself.

Analysis, in common with all medical treatments, is suitable for some cases and not for others. There are two types of analysis, sometimes designated as symptom-analysis and character-analysis. The former, as its name suggests, is useful in helping to remove specific neurotic symptoms, such as claustrophobia, hysterical muscular contraction, and conditions which during war came under the broad classification of shell-shock. These often, but by no means always, yield to a short period of treatment of from three to six months and occasionally less.

Character-analysis is a much larger question. It may take several years, with perhaps intermittent treatment in the later stages, and may involve very profound psychological readjustments. Such treatment is far from suitable for everyone who happens to be unhappy and maladjusted. For certain types it may be disintegrating. For those who have not reached a stage in their development where they are capable of making a conscious alignment with the higher self, there is a very real danger of analysing down to the automatic level of the purely instinctual life rather than using the treatment as the preliminary step towards a conscious re-integration of the whole man. This is one of the dangers of the purely Freudian or the reductive methods. Reductive analysis, if used, should be the preliminary stage for a positive re-education of the patient leading towards integration with his spiritual self. It must be borne in mind that analysis results in definite psychological changes, whether for good or ill, whether integrating or disintegrating, and that, once made, these changes cannot be laid aside like a useless garment nor can a facile return be made to the *status quo ante.*

For these reasons it is obvious that a very careful selection should be made not only of the person suitable for analysis but also of the analyst.

There is often no need for analytical treatment if home or social circumstances can be adjusted to ease the psychological pressure. In some cases the actual environment can be changed, by removing a child temporarily from its home, introducing a young person to a social club, or making some simple adjustment towards better marital relations, or towards increased understanding of the fact that other people also have their own psychological difficulties and need sympathy and co-operation as much as the patient himself.

Here again it is a matter of breaking a vicious circle of feeling and thought. The circle once broken, the individual can often carry on normally without undue ill health.

People who for various reasons cannot undertake analysis may occasionally be helped by reading some well chosen books on the subject of psychology. But this is definitely a case where a small dose may cure while a big one is likely to kill. To embark on an extensive study of miscellaneous analytical literature, which by hypothesis deals largely with the morbid aspects of the human mind, is one of the worst things a neurotic patient can do.

A few books will be listed in the appendix. The physician who is familiar with them will be able to select those suitable in a given case.[26]

RE-EDUCATION AND AFFIRMATION. Affirmation and suggestion have much in common, but whereas suggestion is usually administered by a practitioner, affirmation implies auto-suggestion and is based upon an old method of self re-education used scientifically in eastern systems of yoga. The New Thought, or Higher Thought, movement has familiarized the West with the practice of affirmation, but unfortunately the practice has frequently been associated with a denial of the existence of pain, as well as with a negation of the reality of physical matter. It also lends itself to shallow application, with obviously superficial reactions. The result may easily be a failure to achieve permanent health, or the acquiring of various unwholesome psychological distortions, so that the last state may on occasion be worse than the first. Yet, at root, the theory is sound. It is a physical fact that a pattern made in sand upon a vibratory disc can be obliterated and shaped afresh by imposing a new rate of vibration upon the disc. All personal experience is associated with vibratory material of suitable degrees of subtlety, thought building the thought-forms, emotion flowing in swirls of emotional matter. Psychological behaviour patterns are therefore visible realities, with characteristic colours and shapes, to clairvoyant sight. The theory is that it is possible to create, for example, the radiating quality of love and goodwill so strongly in one's consciousness that anger and withdrawal are inevitably obliterated, because the vibratory rate of love will overwhelm hostility. So if a student recognizes some harmful attitude in himself, such as worry, fear, etc., in order to overcome it he is to affirm with persistence the exactly opposite quality. Then the old habit will die out, the new gradually becoming dominant and finally habitual.[27]

The principle of substituting a positive quality for its negative opposite is sound if properly understood. Thus if one has a dry well in one's garden, one does not eliminate the hole in the ground by building a lid or tower over it: one fills it in, thus substituting solidity for hollowness. The first is in effect what psychologists call repression or over-compensation, the second is true resolution or transmutation.

In psychic terms, true resolution would mean the breaking up of morbid or inhibiting thought-forms and patterns in the higher bodies, and the actual remodelling of the psychic material into new and more socially constructive arrangements. It is part of this theory to admit the disastrous effects upon health of 'wrong' attitudes and to desire the 'right' because they make for well-being physically as well as spiritually.

Failure in the use of this method, which, in the abstract, is perfectly sound, is due to the fact that the various levels of human consciousness can function independently, and the repeated reverberation of a beautiful idea can continue at its own level without very much affecting the roots of the old psychological state existing at another. In the East there is not so much mental rigidity and separation between the levels of consciousness as in the more materially-minded West, so that the method may be more effective there than here. As in the practice of suggestion, a fixed habit of consciousness defeats the true use of affirmation, for the old pattern is likely to remain fundamentally unaltered and reassert itself at critical moments. For such conditions, the analytical technique may be necessary in order to get within the charmed circle of the old habit.

Thus, for the western mind, it is frequently beneficial to prepare for the use of affirmation by looking frankly back at the past, allowing the past to reconstruct itself in such a way that it may be relived and accepted as an integral part of one's storehouse of experience. In order to integrate the past to one's current views it may indeed be necessary to relive it, and this frequently happens in confidential talks with doctors and of course in analytical interviews. If, however, a patient is able really to see the past afresh, and to accept it reasonably, there is no need to relive it, and certainly no necessity for repeated interviews dwelling upon past miseries and failures. The acceptance of the past implies becoming unafraid of it, or of the continued re-emergence of the psychological states involved, e.g. panic, shame, anger, jealousy, resentment, etc. Such feelings may recur, but the patient can now handle, and in the end, assimilate them.

Once a conscious break in the old fixed habit can be effected by these or any other means, then a deliberate use of affirmation is of the greatest value in undermining the whole complex. The lack of some active therapy of this nature is one common reason for the failure of analytical treatments to make people happy and creative. There are also times when the psychological attitude that is being attacked is so deeply embedded in the fabric of the unconscious that the will must be invoked in order to make a free and repeated choice of the new habit which the patient now deliberately chooses to cultivate.[28]

The practice of continued discrimination is needed to distinguish between the mere repression of an undesirable quality and the creative affirmation which is really regenerative. For example, the patient in an accident case who has been badly handled psychologically, and who has developed a firm conviction that he will be unable to do a full day's work for the rest of his life, may be led to understand the factors, both physical and psychological, inhibiting the flow of vitality through his body, and then may make good use of affirmations to bring about a gradual increase of activity in his limbs and nerves. This is a very positive form of auto-suggestion and can have great therapeutic value, for the reasons already given. But if the accident itself was the unconscious result of a deep-seated shirking of responsibility, and the reason for the flight from life has not been uncovered, the improvement may suddenly stop at a critical point, and the deeper analytical technique outlined above will be needed to effect a permanent cure. This whole matter has been admirably dealt with in the novel, *Camberwell Miracle*, by J. D. Beresford, and the student is referred to that.[29]

Gentle re-education, suggestions in regard to reading, the diversion of the mind into other channels, in fact all the old, tried and to-day too little used, common-sense methods of lifting a patient out of a rut into a new flow of life, are all subtle forms of affirmation and suggestion and can be used advantageously in given cases.

VI. SACRAMENTAL AND SPIRITUAL HEALING

Miracles do happen. The patient *in extremis* receives the sacrament of unction, and recovers; the lame man goes to Lourdes, and walks thereafter; the neurotic attends a healing service and becomes permanently normal. The explanation in each case would involve the whole life history of each patient, because the converse is also true: unction rarely heals, many are not cured at Lourdes, neurotics commonly go from one spiritual healer to another and remain neurotics. As J. D. Beresford so ably points out in the book referred to above, it is a certain alignment on the part of the patient, a deep inner acceptance of some new attitude to life, that makes the miracle possible. Naturally, suggestion plays a great part in apparent miracles. Before accepting any case as a miraculous cure, it should be very carefully examined. It is very rare that some other explanation of a more mundane character is not forthcoming. The cancer case cured by laying-on of hands has probably never been proved to be cancer; the consumptive never proved to be tuberculous. On the other hand many miracles one hears of have taken place in cases of obvious conversion hysteria, where physical symptoms are produced unconsciously from emotional causes.

Such things as magnetic healing or therapy by suggestion are often confused with spiritual healing. They are, in fact, nothing of the kind, but belong to a much more mundane level.

The literature available on this subject is as yet scanty and unsatisfactory. Clairvoyants agree that there are healing centres, healing angels and forces of personal magnetism involved in all spiritual healing. Certain great healing personalities seem to act as physical plane foci for hidden forces.[30]

Ritual ceremonies harmonize the bodies of those who can yield themselves to their influence; and atmospheres are created around healers, as well as at sacred places of pilgrimage and places associated with healing in the past, which make it easier for a patient to let go resistance and so be open to the healing influences there present.[31]

In estimating the failure and success of methods of spiritual healing all the complicated forces of karma need to be considered. These are knotted by resistance in antagonistic natures, eased by helpful circumstances and the attitude of self-surrender. A psychic or psychological condition may suddenly reach a climax which brings 'light' to the individual, who can then be healed. A miracle, then, depends upon the patient quite as much as upon the outside agent or place. The problem is one of mutual interplay, and of the capacity of the patient to make use of the healing powers provided by person, place, or ritual.

No.	Page	
1	136	The solid material assists normal elimination.
2	137	R. T. Morris: 50 *Years a Surgeon*. Bles.
3	139	See Appendix: Reading list on Osteopathy.
4	139	*The 1937 Year Book of General Therapeutics*, Ed. B. Fantus, pp. 415-419. H. K. Lewis.
5	142	E. Jacobson: *Progressive Relaxation*. University of Chicago Press.

5   142   E. Jacobson: *Progressive Relaxation*. University of Chicago Press.
E. Jacobson: *You Must Relax* and *You can Sleep Well*. McGraw-Hill.
A. P. Call: *Power Through Repose*. Gay & Hancock.

6   144   O. Leyton: *Treatment of Diabetes Mellitus*, pp. 62, 63. Adlard. Case cited showing difficulty in administration of adrenalin to life-long vegetarian.

7   145   J. A. Silburn M.I.H., etc., *Dieting in Health and Sickness*. Heath & Heather, St. Albans, pp. 43 and 44.

8   145   J. W. Murray: *Examination of the Patient and Symptomatic Diagnosis*, pp. 51-52. Kimptom, 1936.
'A mixed diet insures the greatest amount of health and strength. Certain bacteria are normal in the intestine, but may cause more or less serious symptoms of toxaemia if they become enormously multiplied, or under favourable conditions in the intestine for their growth, produce sufficient toxins to cause the symptoms observed in intestinal indigestion. "Also there may develop in the intestines, bacteria which are absolutely foreign to the intestines, i.e. which are distinctly pathologic. It has also been shown that certain bacteria thrive best on protein digestive products, or rather on the products of protein indigestion, and if this pabulum is removed, the germs die a natural death. This same is true of certain germs that grow best in the carbohydrate by-products or digestive products, and, here again, if this pabulum is changed, the germs die. The cause of putrefaction in the intestines of adults is more likely to be the result of protein decomposition. This knowledge is not utilized as frequently as it should be, in the treatment of these intestinal indigestions. . . .
"Rapid changes in the diets of men, monkeys, and cats, from a dominant protein diet to one in which carbohydrates predominate, are followed by definite and consistent changes in physiologic conditions in three definite directions, viz: (*a*) In the nature of the bacterial flora. (*b*) In the putrefactive products of the faeces and urine. (*c*) In the clinical conditions." Osborne: *Handbook of Therapy*.'

No.	Page	
9	148	B. Macfadden: *Fasting for Health*. Macfadden Publications, New York.
10	148	J. S. Bainbridge: *Diet for the Million*. Williams and Norgate.
11	149	London Vegetarian Society, 9 Adam Street, W.C.2. R. M. Le Quesne and M. Granville: *Hydrotherapy*. Cassell.
12	150	E. Powell: *Water Treatments*, Chaps. IV and V. E. W. Daniel.
13	151	Op. cit., Chap. V.
14	153	C. E. Iredell: *Colour and Cancer*. H. K. Lewis.
15	153	J. Dodson Hessey: *Colour in the Treatment of Disease*. Rider. E. D. Babbitt: *The Principles of Light and Colour*, 1896. Kegan Paul & Trench.
16	154	A. Gardner: *Vital Magnetic Healing*. Theosophical Research Centre. See also *Camberwell Miracle*, a novel by J. D. Beresford. Heinemann.
17	158	Kogh and others: Report of a Discussion on Growth Factors, at the Royal Society, June 24th, 1937. *Nature*, July 24th, 1937. Nielsen and Hartelius, *Nature*, August 1st, p. 203. J. Russell: Report of lecture on 'Applications of Chemistry to Modern Food Production', *Nature*, Vol. CXXXIX, June, 1937, p. 974.
18	158	See Appendix: Reading list on Homoeopathy.
19	159	E. Powell: *Biochemic Pocket Book*. Stonham.
20	161	See section on Special Techniques, p. 115.
21	163	J. T. Kent: *Homoeopathic Philosophy*, p. 23. Eckhart & Kent, 1919.
22	163	See under neck and throat in lists of Correspondences, p. 125.
23	165	G. Dick Read: *Natural Childbirth*. Heinemann.
24	167	See homoeopathic literature on this point.
25	174	Geraldine Coster: *Yoga and Western Psychology*, Chap. XIII. Oxford University Press.
26	180	See Appendix: Reading list on Psychotherapy.
27	180	A. Besant: *Thought Power*, Chap. IX. Theosophical Publishing House, London.
28	182	*A Challenge to Neurasthenia*, Anon. Williams & Norgate.
29	183	See also J. D. Beresford: *The Case for Faith Healing*. Allen & Unwin.
30	184	H. S. Olcott, the first President of the Theosophical Society, apparently was such a focus for about two years. The record of the many remarkable cures effected by him during this period is interesting reading. H. S. Olcott: *Old Diary Leaves*, Vol. II. Theosophical Publishing House, London.
31	184	See Appendix: Reading list on Spiritual Healing.

Chapter VII

NOTES ON SPECIAL DISEASES

W E do not need to consider further the ordinary run of diseases. There are, however, certain puzzling diseases, such as eczema, asthma, allergic conditions, and certain post-anaesthetic conditions, which are often inadequately treated, and require different methods than those usually applied. Examples of methods which have been found useful in such diseases will therefore be outlined, both because the actual diseases cited have responded especially well to the treatments indicated and also because a few examples will be useful to illustrate the application in clinical work of the principles in this book. The chapter will conclude with a group of selected cases illustrating points which have recurred throughout the book.

ALLERGY originally indicated over-reactivity to specific toxin-producing substances to which ordinary people remain immune, e.g. the pollen of certain plants, which in the case of certain individuals apparently induces hay fever. Its connotation has now been enlarged, and it indicates the tendency to give abnormal or exaggerated responses to any substance, reactions to which are otherwise normally predictable. Where allergy exists, i.e. when people give an allergic response to certain stimuli, both under and over-reactions occur extremely unexpectedly; for example, a child's dose of Antikamnia may produce delirium in an adult, or the eating of a few strawberries cause nettle-rash.

Etiology. The causes of these unpredictable responses may be classed as follows: The general basis of allergic reactions is a disturbed or distorted vital matrix, or double, which has in some one of many ways, or in all of them, had its balance and pattern disturbed. Being in a special state of unstable equilibrium it can be acutely upset and give what may be called an hysterical reaction, either exaggeratedly negative or positive, on extremely slight provocation. The causes of this condition in the vital body can be at any level of consciousness or may be the result of a combination of strains at different points.

(a) It is sometimes caused by *special physiological conditions*, such as those which arise in many vegetarians who are also non-smokers and total abstainers. With such a régime the blood stream may become very sensitive to stimulants, depressants, and indeed to any strong drug. An ordinary massive dose of tonic has been known to act as a poison for such individuals, and they generally react better to homoeopathic remedies or to a child's dose of allopathic remedies. Many vegetarians give an allergic reaction to meat, even when taken unwittingly in food thought to be vegetarian.

(b) Secondary conditions of active or suppressed toxaemia may arise in some individuals who have been over-dosed with *unsuitable medicines*, e.g. aspirin taken continually, mercury, quinine, etc. Protein shock from certain modern medicines, e.g. bacterial vaccines, sera, and some gland extracts, is recognized as a cause of allergic reactions, either immediately, or, in cases of anaphylaxis, considerably later. There can be an actual poisoning of certain tissues or a general abnormality of the blood stream. In the latter instance the blood is not so much actually poisoned as suffering from a disturbance of its electrical field; hence its behaviour becomes erratic.

(c) *Psychic and psychological factors.* Whereas (a) and (b) mentioned above disturb the double through its association with the physical body, psychic and psychological disturbance of a subtle and long-continued nature can affect it in spite of the maintenance of an excellent physical régime. For example, a child may develop eczema through association with highly nervous or overwhelming parents. The state of psychological tension in which the child exists registers in a frayed vital body that is literally 'scratchy' with tension and so fails to function normally; this is at once communicated to the nerves of the physical skin. Such cases do not respond well to purely physical treatment.

Psychic children, who often feel themselves to be 'odd' and 'different', and psychic adults as well, tend to give allergic reactions to all treatments. Hysterics, whose vital bodies are usually in a state of abnormal tension, also frequently react allergically to tonics, sedatives, anaesthetics, etc. The condition or disease in all these cases is genuine. Such people are not merely imaginative or perverse. They have produced in themselves a state of nerve tension which is destructive to vital tone, and the vital body becomes frayed, over-extended, inert or inchoate, according to the physiological or psychological type.

Treatments Advised. Very little medicine is needed and then only of the simplest.[1] Relaxation, breathing, should be taught, and any useful exercises which are rhythmic or creative and take the attention from the body, e.g. gardening, walking in pleasant scenery, swimming. Coloured light and magnetic treatment are helpful if available. Careful attention should be given to diet, which should be simple, vital and attractive. The patient needs to be led to assume that he has the capacity to develop more normal reactions, through the use of simple physical exercises and the cultivation of better relationships with his environment. Children's environment usually must be adjusted to them if cure of a specific condition, such as eczema, is to be assured.

In general, the patient must be very carefully studied, tension relieved, and a new and better vital habit gradually induced. Such individuals will always need specially considered treatment.

DIABETES. *Etiology.* Clairvoyant diagnosis reveals that the spleen chakram is always blocked in this disease, and the spleen itself is frequently affected; the pancreas is also involved, and a condition of imbalance exists between the para-sympathetic nervous system, especially the vagus nerve, and the sympathetic nervous system, affecting particularly the nerves in the immediate area of the solar plexus chakram.

There may be, and often is, a great over-stimulation of the activity of the sympathetic nervous system due to *psychological attitudes which foster this disease*, or, at the other extreme, a stasis of parts of this system, with consequent unregulated activity of the organs mentioned, due originally to direct over-tension and later to exhaustion after long-continued stimulus. In the latter case the autonomic ganglion associated with the solar plexus chakram becomes deadened and inactive. It is interesting that the disease is found to be more common among Jews than Gentiles, and it is also very common in a mild form among natives of India and Ceylon. Emotional disturbance occurs readily in these peoples, and this over-strains the solar plexus area. The other type that tends to develop this disease is one deeply withdrawn from life and refusing to make ordinary contacts.

Treatment. When patients are able to respond to suggestion and psychological advice they should be led to accept life *as it is.* If the psyche is sufficiently adult in development to be induced to do this, a profound change in metabolism can result. Otherwise a substitution of more congenial occupation, giving more stimulus to thought or to more contented feelings, is essential. This may prevent the establishment of the disease if taken early enough. Once it is well rooted, however, there is no alternative to the accepted and usual method of treatment.

Diet. The diets elaborated by modern research are good. They include a reduction of carbohydrates rather than complete deletion.[2]

Insulin. This drug is now recognized as substitutional rather than curative, and should be used as may be found necessary. Some doctors prescribe yeast, as possessing a ferment comparable to insulin, but its value is doubtful.

Homoeopathic medication has various constitutional remedies, depending more on the patient than the disease, the effect of which is to undermine the tendency and restore metabolic balance. These constitutional remedies should be used here, as in all other chronic conditions, as a routine basic approach to the metabolic problem.

ASTHMA and other allergic diseases, including urticaria; also bronchitis when caused by irritant fumes or accompanying chronic asthma. *Etiology.* Seen clairvoyantly, the root problem is acute though very subtle vital tension. The throat chakram is nearly always distorted, the heart chakram sometimes. If there is mental strain, the brow chakram is also affected. Osteopathic lesions are usually present, probably in the upper thoracic region, or of the fourth and fifth cervical vertebrae, permitting the vagus nerve to become over active through the inhibition of the sympathetic nerves of the pulmonary plexus.

Psychological Correspondence.[3] Frequently, acute fear of some aspect of life, usually at a deeply unconscious level, and in most cases further hidden by a tendency to rationalization and to the avoidance of disagreeable situations. The reverse attitude of over-conscientiousness, hypercriticism, and over eagerness may also bring about the same condition, and the two attitudes may exist side by side. Tension is the keynote.

Treatments. Osteopathy should be used when indicated, and always there is need for education in relaxation and normal breathing. Diet is important, with special regard to assimilation of proteins and to digestive malfunction in general, e.g. certain asthmatics are benefited by regular doses of dilute hydrochloric acid at meal times. Adrenalin may be necessary for acute paroxysms, also, in serious cases, ephedrin and opiates, because they relax the basic vital tension.

Psychological Treatments. Suggestion and re-education are necessary in order to relieve the subtle psychic and psychological strain which is causing the tension. The asthmatic type is often very resistant to analysis, but sometimes responds well to the right kind of suggestion.

CERTAIN POST-ANAESTHETIC CONDITIONS: Poisoning, collapse, and failure to return to normal consciousness.

Anaesthesia is due to the effects of certain drugs upon the vital body. General anaesthesia affects the whole vital body, particularly that part which acts as the bridge between the inner or real man and the brain consciousness. In local anaesthesia, local portions of the vital structure are displaced. The effect of an anaesthetic is to produce a condition in the physical cells, particularly in those of the nervous system, which disconnects the vital counterpart from the dense physical cells in such a way that communication of physical stimuli can no longer be carried over to the interior consciousness. In normal sleep somewhat the same effect is produced by the withdrawal of consciousness from the physical body, this withdrawal tending to displace the vital counterpart, so that the inner consciousness is largely undisturbed by physical occurrences. Under anaesthetics the vital body is actually driven out from the physical by the drug administered, and the severance is far more complete. Thus, when anaesthetic drugs displace the vital body, the result is a literal lifting of a drawbridge of tenuous matter out of the brain or nerve cells or fibres. This drawbridge, the connecting vital material, is left hanging down from, or slightly on one side of, the part affected.

Individual reactions to an anaesthetic differ according to (1) the type of the patient's vital body; (2) the psychological attitude of the patient; (3) the form of anaesthetic or anaesthetics, i.e. volatile and/or non-volatile.

(1) The dense vital type is slow in throwing off results and recuperating. The fluid type is easily poisoned or dislocated at the vital level, but the reactions are largely determined by the psychological attitude; recurring sickness is usual. The fiery types take volatile anaesthetics easily. In the airy, bland type no specially defined tendencies have been observed.

These are generalizations only, and given individuals

are frequently not true to type because of psychological or other influences.

(2) The psychological problem involved in taking an anaesthetic is so complex that only one or two especially significant points can be dealt with here. Resistance to the anaesthetic can be due to fear of losing consciousness, fear of surrender, fear of the unknown, of death, etc. It is of major importance to reduce this resistance to a minimum, although this is not always possible. If time permits, the patient should be taught to relax the physical body, to breathe quietly and rhythmically, etc. Suggestion at the time of administering the anaesthetic is very useful, such as suggestion that the patient think of something pleasant at a distance. The projection of vital material from the body is actually facilitated by thinking of oneself as away from the immediate environment. The relation of the vital body to the dense physical under anaesthesia has something in common with that produced by deeply dissociated psychological states, such as those caused by profound psychological shock. It is important to note this, as an anaesthetic administered to an already dissociated person may have abnormal results. Dissociated states of consciousness vary from a relatively superficial and temporary condition, due to physical shock only, to a long-standing and deep-seated state of retreat from life which has associated with it an actual rift in the psychic structure. In the first instance a person who has just been involved in an accident and who is, therefore, severely shocked psychologically as well as physically, should be dealt with as a special case, because of the cumulative effect of one shock on another. In the other, the person who wishes to die or to withdraw from life may take the anaesthetic well, and need little, but may recover slowly, because there is a mental-emotional bias in the direction of unconsciousness. Between these two extreme examples are any number of variations in psychologically dissociated conditions with a corresponding variety of reactions to anaesthetics.

N

Under this heading there is need to consider individuals of marked psychic tendencies, whether the psychic faculty be consciously used or not, because persons of this type have peculiarly constructed vital bodies that are readily dispersed by the use of any kind of anaesthetic.

The psychic who is positive to his psychic perceptions, and also the self-aware artist, have a general tendency to exaggerated vital dislocation, arising from extreme oversensitiveness to all stimuli. Such a tendency to dislocation may be enhanced by an anaesthetic although this reaction does not necessarily always occur. The person who is negatively psychic is the most uncertain of all in his reactions and has a definite tendency to react badly. Psychics can belong to any psychological or vital type and their behaviour under anaesthetics will be modified by the consequent differences in the vital structure.

(3) Clairvoyant observation notes a clearly defined difference in the effect upon the vital structure of volatile and non-volatile anaesthetics, although, owing to lack of opportunity, these observations have usually been made some time after actual administration. Where a volatile anaesthetic is used, poisoning of tissues rarely occurs, because of the rapid elimination. An accentuated dislocation of the vital body can occur, however, through the actual dissipation or disintegration of etheric material in certain localities where there is a special psychological pressure or nervous strain, e.g. solar plexus. The chakras are deeply affected by volatile anaesthetics and can even be temporarily paralysed. Shock and excessive vomiting always increase dislocation of the chakras and also of the vital body as a whole. Some patients are very slow in recovering consciousness in any case, because their vital structure reassembles slowly. This, as we have noted, is particularly likely to occur in psychologically dissociated types with already overstrained vital bodies, or when a basal anaesthetic has first been given and poisoning of the vital body resulted. Non-volatile anaesthetics very deeply

affect the denser vital structure associated with the nerves. On the other hand, they are quickly eliminated through the kidneys and, because they do not so much affect the subtler vital functions, are often better tolerated than, say, ether, by sensitive people. Yet basal anaesthetics have a predilection for nerve tissue, and sometimes are very slowly eliminated from the nervous system and corresponding vital structures. This reaction is much more marked in certain types than in others, for some can throw off the poison fairly easily, others retain it for months, and then an actual poisoning of nerve centres can result. While the poison remains the vital body in that area lacks co-ordination and its texture is altered.

The effects noted above should be carefully watched in relation to the advantages gained by the use of basal anaesthetics in avoiding psychic shock and minimizing the amount of volatile anaesthetic necessary.

Treatments. (a) For collapse, and failure to return to normal consciousness immediately after an operation, give vital magnetic treatment to cleanse the vital body and to start prānic circulation, particularly around the heart and solar plexus. The usual saline technique may be used, preferably by the rectum rather than subcutaneously or intravenously, also the usual stimulants. Pituitrin is to be avoided, for choice, as it also has acute reactions upon vital co-ordination, and may exaggerate rather than help the disorganized state of the vital body. Frequent doses of glucose are useful.

(b) In cases of *slow recovery*, post-anaesthetic conditions of weakness, loss of memory, etc., the vital structure is probably dislocated at some point. Vital magnetic treatment, again, is indicated, especially to the solar plexus chakram and to the back of the neck; also blue light, not too dark or intense. Gentle massage is sometimes effective when the above are not available. Homoeopathic remedies, e.g. arnica 30 and others, act directly upon the vital body and are occasionally successful; for this purpose the low and middle potencies, not the high, are better. Reassurance and expectant treatment should be used, with light diet but by no means fruit only.

This condition may be prolonged, even to years. Similar conditions also occur in the case of severe reactions to labour in childbirth. If long continued, use rose light, relaxation, good easy breathing, massage or magnetic treatment, suggestion and affirmation. Osteopathy is occasionally indicated when the spine has been very much relaxed and may have become maladjusted. This frequently happens to the atlas or cervical vertebrae.

Psychological treatment to induce readjustment is sometimes necessary. If there is a predisposing psychological attitude underlying abnormal reactions to anaesthetics, post-anaesthetic conditions lend themselves readily as a screen to both conscious and unconscious retreat or unwillingness to handle the problems likely to arise on recovery.

The statement of the patient that he is 'longing to get well, Doctor,' does not preclude the presence of this factor.

NOTES AND REFERENCES FOR CHAPTER VII

No. Page

1   189   'The administration of gland extracts in order to relieve acute symptoms, as advised in orthodox textbooks, cannot be held to be in any sense curative, and may even be adding to the basic disturbance of function from which the allergic reactions arise.'

        Textbook and Practice of Medicine, p. 730. Ed. F. W. Price. Oxford University Press, 1933.

2   190   Op. cit., p. 438.

3   191   J. L. Halliday: 'The Approach to Asthma'. *British Journal of Medical Psychology*, Vol. XVII, Part 1, October, 1937.

Chapter VIII

CONCLUSION

IT may seem at first sight that the scheme of man put forward in this book is extremely complicated, and only adds further difficulties to a view of man already complex enough. In fact, it is less complicated, because it is concerned with generalities regarding certain sections of the total organism, and not with the overwhelming mass of detail, physiological, histological and biochemical which turns modern medicine into an almost impenetrable jungle.

In giving the details of this picture of man we have described at some length the delicate vital organism by which thought and feeling register their influences in the glands, nerves and tissues of the dense physical frame, and we have attempted to show the relation of the vital mechanism not only to general health, but also to such conditions as post-anaesthetic shock, prolonged exhaustion and dissociated mental states.

Following the indications suggested by the view of man which sees him to be body, psyche and spirit, we have also attempted to outline an approach to the problems of disease causation, diagnosis and treatment, which includes a consideration of all three of these factors. This view, however, has much in common with the best of modern therapeutic theory and practice. The tendency to-day in treating all forms of nervous and functional disorder is to lay more and more emphasis upon the underlying psychological factors. Furthermore, the problem of resistance to disease is also beginning to be linked with a study of those attitudes of mind which conduce to a healthy tone of bodily activity as well as of those on the other hand, such as anxiety, fear, etc., which are understood to be disintegrative in their effect.

We would go further, however, and say that pioneer research workers are making out a good case for a drastic re-consideration of the whole bacterial theory, and that the medical mind is becoming detached from its limpet-like adherence to the concept that diseases are caused by the invasion of specific micro-organisms, and is turning to the consideration of the underlying causes which determine the varying development of the bacterial forms.

There is a marked forward movement in medical theory and practice. But to substitute biochemistry or even psychology for the bacterial theory is not enough, because it still leaves out the fundamental cause of man's very existence—the spiritual Self.

In the chapter on diagnosis there is much of which the most up-to-date students will approve, and where we have ventured into new territory, as in the list of correspondences between psychological and physiological disorders, we put forward our findings tentatively, for what they may be worth, and to provoke observation and experiment on the part of others.

In the long chapter on treatments and in the following one on special diseases there is probably a great deal that will be challenged by those who are enthusiastic believers in injections and gland therapy. This challenge is to be expected and goes to the root of the matter. We are on the whole opposed, except in emergency, to all forms of treatment based upon the administration of extraneous substitutes for substances which the body should normally produce for itself. We favour methods which provoke normal function, while seeking the causes of malfunction at the vital and psychic levels. Substitutes for the normal secretions of the body may at best produce a temporary alleviation of symptoms and so permit readjustment to occur, but their dangers and uncertainties are more and more admitted by all honest observers in the medical world.

We are fully aware that there are certain subjects which

we have neglected to consider. One of these is the need for distinction between psychological and purely psychic conditions in neurotic and over-sensitized patients. While the psychological factors in certain nervous states are beginning to be understood by specialists in psychotherapy, conditions of actual objective psychic experience are still not recognized, nor has any acknowledged technique been developed either for training psychic capacity so that it may be useful in research work, or for distinguishing between its healthy and its morbid manifestations. This subject is omitted here for two reasons. The first is that we need far more time to consider the problems involved if we are to contribute anything more than a superficial view of so unusual and complicated a study; and the second is that even were the material available we do not think that it would be suitable to include it here. It is a problem for psychotherapists and psychiatrists and requires separate treatment.

The same points hold good in regard to the application of the principles we have outlined to such specific problems as obstetrics. Excellent obstetrical work is being done on these lines indicated (see Chapter VI, Reference No. 25), but it is a subject in itself and cannot be developed here.

There are years of work waiting to be done upon the study of the vital body, its resistance or susceptibility to contagion and its reactions to psychological and physiological fatigue, etc. Much more detail is needed to add to our knowledge of the reactions of the subtler bodies to psychological states, induced both subjectively by the patient and externally by circumstances. If only the attention of orthodox research students could be turned in this direction, much could be established by western methods of research which would be of the greatest importance in developing therapeutic technique. For such work assistance from trained clairvoyants is of the greatest help and so is a confident use of disciplined intuitive perception. One of the present difficulties in research work is that when instruments are evolved of sufficient sensitivity to register the reactions of the vital body—instruments such as certain psychogalvanometers and other types of apparatus that react to the electromagnetic conditions around the human body—the results which occur are completely confusing to most observers because they have no intelligible concept of what it is that is being recorded. For example, in a few preliminary experiments with this type of apparatus which this group has carried out it was found that certain loosely knit or somewhat heavier vital bodies, usually those of types 1 or 2, could set a sensitive circuit oscillating erratically just by their presence, whereas the other vital types might only be able to affect such a circuit by deliberately directing the flow of vitality across the circuit through an effort of concentrated thought. Again, an emotional uprush in a closely knit vital type may cause very little disturbance in the instrument, but a minor confusion at the feeling level in a subject with a loosely knit vital body may register as a considerable movement of the indicator. Without some knowledge of vital types, and of the variations in structure of the subtler bodies, research students are naturally bewildered, and we hope that this book may fall into the hands of some workers in Parapsychology and Psychical Research, who will be sufficiently open-minded at least to examine those of its implications that bear upon psychological research work.

In this connection attention should be drawn once more to the work of Dr. Thérèse Brosse and Professor J. E. Marcault of Paris, who by using an electro-cardiogram, and studying the reactions of the heart, etc., to mental-emotional conditions as well as those induced by yogis in trance, have furnished us with certain very satisfactory data regarding the relation of human consciousness to the physical body (see Chapter III, References 9 and 30).

In conclusion may we again emphasize the basic difference between the approach that we have indicated and that of materialistic medicine. In accepting the spatial nature of the bodies of thought and feeling, and in making an attempt to understand the interrelation of these bodies with the functioning of man's physical organism, a totally different approach to the whole problem of health and disease is implied—not merely an increased stress upon the importance of certain psychological factors. On all sides to-day persons of renown in the medical world are beginning to realize and to discuss in public the necessity for the inclusion of psychological factors in the study of health and disease. With a few exceptions, however, such speakers admit the psyche into the medical field as a useful adjunct to an already established science, a science which regards the physical organism as complete in itself, with psychological influences impinging upon it in a rather extraneous fashion. For our part, envisaging man as a whole—spirit, soul and body—this relationship is entirely reversed. Man's nature is recognized as springing from a spiritual centre, upon which centre the organs of thought, feeling and action all depend for their integrated existence. The play of environment, heredity and all physical circumstances upon the physical body, and hence back into the psyche, is already known; whereas the immense significance of the flow of life from the spirit and the psyche outwards should be more fully appreciated and understood. If the ancient art of healing is to be restored to its true place, man must be studied as a whole and medical, psychological and spiritual factors seen, not in incidental association, but as combined in a functioning unity.

Moreover, the basic causes of health and of disease will never be laid bare while we seek to understand them through observing variation in the development of micro-organisms which have been artificially implanted in the blood and tissues of rabbits and guinea pigs. Man is a host who shelters myriads of these organisms within his frame, and according to the nourishment supplied by their host, the food he gives them, the rest or disturbance they experience while under his care, they pass their existence harmlessly or turn and rend him. The behaviour of bacteria in people of varying temperaments, at various seasons of the year, under varying conditions of contentment and stress, needs deep investigation. If the ancient teachings are sound, as they appear to us to be, the state of integration or disintegration of the tri-partite individual will be found to be the basic problem of the physician as of the psychologist.

When the real relation of man's thinking and feeling to his health is fully seen, preventive medicine also will enter a new phase. Individual doctors, as well as Departments of Public Health and medical bodies everywhere, are becoming more and more interested in hygiene, in fitness and in the social application of preventive medicine. Yet so long as the purely materialistic view of man and of society is accepted, fitness campaigns may too often hinge upon the need for able-bodied soldiers and these will later on be inoculated, vaccinated and 'anti-bodied' against all comers. On the other hand once the source of variation in bacterial development has been recognized and the importance of psychological states in the maintenance of immunity admitted, the very reasons for seeking fitness will also have to undergo a change.

Distinguished scientists to-day, in order to reach satisfactory conclusions in regard to the deeper problems of nature, have included metaphysical considerations in the field of their work. It is but natural that, in attempting to solve the problem of health in the human individual, man's unseen activities should be admitted as significant and their import studied. A progressive integration of the individual can only very rarely be achieved on the basis of the strictly materialistic view of human existence.

We would suggest that the encouragement of health, or genuine wholeness, on the part of any group or nation, if honestly pursued will, in the end, lead to the acknowledgment of the significance of unseen and hitherto unrecognized factors of the utmost importance. In winning or losing a long drawn out or subtle fight against death it is the unexpected, the physically imponderable factors that determine the issue, and it is to these little recognized and very little studied imponderables that we trust this book will draw the attention of students and of research workers, as well as that of the specialist and of the family physician.

The Dying Patient

A problem which confronts everybody at times is that of imminent death. The non-medical onlooker can do little except stand by and perhaps give moral support, but the doctor in particular, and the nurses in a secondary way, have the responsibility of dealing with the situation according to the best of their abilities.

When faced with a patient at the point of death, three courses of action are possible: to try to prolong life; to consider first and foremost the comfort of the patient; or to kill the patient in a painless way. There is a fourth course, which is to adopt a negative, fatalistic attitude and do nothing but let events take their course.

The last two can be eliminated at once. For to stand aside and do nothing is to neglect one's duty as a physician. To kill, on the other hand, is a thing which only a materialist who feels justified in ignoring the laws of the country and the commandments of religion can justify. One is thus left with the possible alternatives between trying to prolong life even at the cost of suffering to the patient; or of seeing to it that the patient has a minimum amount of pain even though the drugs used may bring death nearer.

Clearly, every case needs to be judged on its merits. But if one believes in the spiritual nature of man, one must respect him as an individual, entitled within wide limits to choose for himself what is to be done to him and his body when sick. This is a principle which can guide one in the matter of the treatment of the moribund.

Three imaginary cases can be considered. The first, that of a young and vigorous man of thirty with lobar pneumonia and pleurisy. He may be suffering a great deal of discomfort, to relieve which dangerous doses of opiates might be required. The patient may even be so depressed that he asks to be put out of his misery at any cost. But the physician knows that if the crisis passes, the patient will get well and be able to carry on a normal and active life for the next thirty or forty years. In such case, obviously, the price of suffering is worth while, and to accede to a request for relief which might cause unnecessary risk of death would be virtually to be an accessory to suicide.

On the other hand, one may have to deal with a patient with inoperable cancer or advanced heart disease. That person has put his affairs in order, the relatives have been seen and the patient has much pain. In such a case it seems not only justifiable, but one's duty, to administer sedatives to the amount needed to procure relief from pain. The patient, already doomed, may die a little earlier because of the treatment given, but he is just as likely to live longer because the strain has been diminished.

Another somewhat similar instance is where a really old person, perhaps already weak, feels that he has reached the end of his days. Maybe he has, so to speak, let go from within himself and sinks into serious illness and has considerable distress. By the constant use of stimulants life might be prolonged for days or even weeks. But—and this does happen in fact—the patient makes a considered judgment and a calm statement that he will be happy to die, and that he does not wish to be galvanised to further effort by artificial means. This situation is quite another from that of the temporarily distracted young man with pneumonia, and one should not disregard the choice made by the patient. Under such circumstances, the doctor's duty is probably to make the patient as comfortable as possible, using drugs if need be to relieve symptoms, and assisting nature to make the passing as easy as possible. He should, moreover, remember that the patient is the one who has the right to decide the matter, rather than give way either to convention or to the selfishness of relatives.

In all cases, commonsense is required. But respect for the individual as a spiritual being, having a measure of freewill, and therefore commanding respect, should be the keynote.

INDEX

MORE BOOKS ON THE SAME SUBJECT

THE MYSTERY OF HEALING

by The Medical Group of The Theosophical
Research Centre, London.

A discussion of the conditions which allow exceptional
cures to take place or which seem to prevent them.

THE PATH OF HEALING

by H. K. Challoner

A description of the true nature and function of
spiritual healing.

— also available —

— a 45 minute cassette tape —

MEDICAL DIAGNOSIS BY CLAIRVOYANCE

by Phoebe and Dr. Laurence Bendit

Questions and answers on the validity and usefulness
of diagnosis by extra-sensory means.